the BULLIES of WALL ST

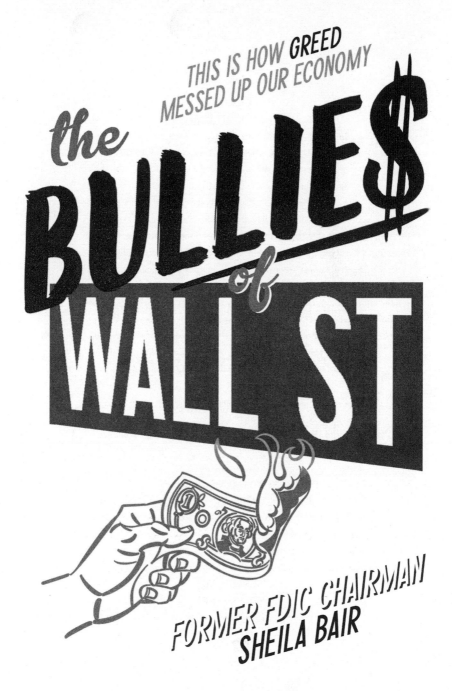

THIS IS HOW GREED
MESSED UP OUR ECONOMY

the BULLIE$ of WALL ST

FORMER FDIC CHAIRMAN
SHEILA BAIR

SIMON & SCHUSTER BFYR

New York   London   Toronto   Sydney   New Delhi

SIMON & SCHUSTER BFYR

An imprint of Simon & Schuster Children's Publishing Division
1230 Avenue of the Americas, New York, New York 10020

For information about special discounts for bulk purchases, please contact Simon &
Schuster Special Sales at 1-866-506-1949 or business@simonandschuster.com.

The Simon & Schuster Speakers Bureau can bring authors to your live event. For
more information or to book an event, contact the Simon & Schuster Speakers
Bureau at 1-866-248-3049 or visit our website at www.simonspeakers.com.

Book design by Lucy Ruth Cummins
The text for this book is set in Adobe Caslon Pro.
Manufactured in the United States of America
2 4 6 8 10 9 7 5 3 1
Library of Congress Cataloging-in-Publication Data
Bair, Sheila
The Bullies of Wall Street: this is how greed messed up our economy/
Sheila Bair
pages cm
ISBN 978-1-4814-0085-5 (hardcover)
ISBN 978-1-4814-0087-9 (eBook)
1. United States—Economic conditions—2001–2009—Juvenile literature.
2. Working class—United States—Economic conditions—Juvenile literature.
3. Financial crises—United States—History—21st century—Juvenile literature.
4. Global Financial Crisis, 2008-2009—Social aspects—Juvenile literature. I. Title
HC106.83.B35 2015
330.973'0931—dc23
2014005948

Dedicated to the young victims of the financial crisis and all the parents, grandparents, teachers, and other loved ones who tried to protect them.

ACKNOWLEDGMENTS

I have many people to thank for inspiring this book and helping me research its content. First, as always, my family—my husband, Scott, and children, Preston and Colleen, for their support and encouragement. Thanks in particular to Colleen, who, at age fourteen, was my in-house sounding board in finding ways to make the financial crisis understandable and interesting to young adults. Thanks also go to Eileen and Jerry Spinelli, whose own books have inspired millions of children and young adults, for urging me to write this book and for suggesting that I use stories describing how young people were hurt by the financial crisis as a way of making it relevant to youthful readers. Thanks also to Rich Brown, Chief Economist at the FDIC, who volunteered his own time with editing and fact checking, and to MIT's Simon Johnson, former Chief Economist of the IMF, for his thoughtful review of the manuscript and helpful suggestions. Thanks also to Stanford's John Taylor, and the staff of the Richmond Federal Reserve Bank, for their help in reviewing the discussions of monetary policy for technical accuracy. Thanks to Dan Arellano and Mark Klupt, of the Boston Consulting Group, for assisting with research, and to Ann Todd and Kathryn Bonk, for assistance in scheduling interviews. I must also express my appreciation to Michael Calhoun at the Center for Responsible Lending, Kevin Whelan, of the Home Defenders League, and the wonderful staff of Operation Hope, for all their help in putting me in touch with families impacted by the crisis. But my greatest gratitude goes to Carmen Pittman, Gisele Mata, Javier Sarmiento, Deborah Castillo, Chaundra Saylor, and all the others who wished to remain anonymous, for taking time to talk with me. Their courage and experiences helped inspire the fictional tales contained in this book.

And of course, final thanks to my editor at Simon & Schuster, Zareen Jaffery, and her team, for all their help bringing this book to fruition.

Sheila Bair
October 2014

CONTENTS

PART 2
MY STORY

INTRODUCTION

In 2008 our country went through a terrible financial crisis. Our financial system, which is supposed to provide responsible loans to families to buy things like houses and cars, or to businesses to buy equipment or hire and pay workers. But in 2008, it stopped working properly. Millions of people lost their homes, their jobs, and much of their life savings. More than 100,000 businesses went bankrupt. Young people were hurt as much as anyone when they were forced to leave their homes and say good-bye to their neighborhood friends, make sacrifices when their parents lost their jobs, experience school cutbacks, cope with lost college savings, and witness untold numbers of their friends and neighbors who confronted the same kind of financial hardships.

The following book is divided into three sections. The first recounts stories of the various ways that kids were hurt by the financial crisis. Following each of the stories are explanations of why these harmful things happened to them. The stories are all fiction, but they are inspired by real-life experiences of people I interviewed, read about, or witnessed firsthand when I was heading an agency called the Federal Deposit Insurance Corporation, which worked to protect families like yours during the crisis and keep their bank deposits safe.

The second part of the book goes into more detail about the mistakes that big financial institutions made that brought us the crisis, and the mistakes that our government made in regulating those financial institutions. This part is really my story. In it I have sought to let you see and feel my dismay and frustration as the crisis unfolded, to witness the greed and misbehavior of too many financial institutions, and to learn of the government's missed opportunities to stop that behavior and do more to help homeowners.

In the third part of the book I talk about your future. I discuss the lingering effects of the financial crisis that will present challenges for your generation, and the things I think you can do to make our country—and our financial services industry—better.

I have written this book because I want you to understand the kinds of shortsighted, selfish behaviors that brought on the financial crisis, in the hope that when you become an adult, you will not make the same mistakes. Many tragedies in human history have been due to factors beyond our control such as disease, famine, or flood. But the 2008 financial crisis was entirely due to our own mistakes and preoccupation with making a quick buck.

The ancient Chinese philosopher Confucius once said, "Study the past if you would define the future." It has taken our country many years to recover from the financial crisis, and we still struggle with its aftershocks. To define a better, brighter future, your generation needs to understand what happened so you will not let it happen again.

PART 1
MAIN STREET

CHAPTER 1

MATT

Matt felt puffs of warm, wet air hitting his cheek. He opened his eyes and saw the source: a large, shiny black nose just a few inches from his face. Two wide-set brown eyes stared at him intently. Attila had probably been awake for hours, patiently waiting for Matt to get up.

Matt lobbed his arm over the old German shepherd's neck and scratched him behind the ears. Matt's mom usually didn't let Attila sleep with him. But she had given in to Matt's pleas the night before, realizing that it would be the last he would share with his dog.

Matt had never known a day without Attila. His parents had adopted him from a dog shelter twelve years ago, just a few months before Matt was born.

He was a big puppy, with huge paws, which was why Matt's dad, a history teacher, decided to name him after Attila the Hun, the ferocious fifth-century warrior who had conquered much of Europe. Attila eventually grew into his paws, weighing over a hundred pounds, big for a German shepherd. His size was now a problem, as Matt's parents couldn't find a place for them to live that would take a dog of his size. The family was moving soon, and all of the apartments they had looked at either prohibited pets or allowed only small ones.

Matt didn't want to get up. He wanted to lie there forever with his dog, thinking back over all of the good years they had spent together. Attila used to be the fastest and smartest dog of any in his neighborhood, making Matt the envy of every kid on his block. His friends would come to his house and beg for the privilege of throwing sticks for Attila to fetch and watching him perform tricks. The usual "sit," "beg," and "roll over" commands were nothing for Attila. He could climb the ladder of Matt's backyard playground set and slide down the slide. He could jump through a hoola hoop and catch Frisbees six feet in the air. He could play tug-of-war with four kids on the other side of the rope, and still win. He didn't just shake. He high-fived.

But that was when Attila was younger. Attila walked slowly now, suffering from arthritis in his hips, which Dad said was common in shepherds. His hearing was almost gone too, so he could no longer always hear Matt's commands.

Matt started to sob softly, and then came an all-out bawl. He gathered up the old dog's coarse, dry fur in his fist and squeezed. Attila belly-crawled closer to him to lick the salty tears from his cheeks. Who would adopt this old dog, who only had a few years left? Who would take in this deaf fellow, who sometimes had accidents in the house and needed help going up and down the stairs? Matt's parents had assured him that the shelter would find a good home for Attila. But Matt had read in the newspaper that lots of families like his were losing their homes and having to give up their pets. The shelters had too many dogs for adoption already. After a time, when they ran out of room, they had to put some "to sleep," which was a nice way of saying that they gave the dogs drugs that made their hearts stop.

Why did they have to move at all? Matt loved their house, with its big fenced-in backyard. He had lived there his entire life. He loved his upstairs bedroom, with the window that overlooked a maple tree that his dad said was a hundred years old. In the summer that tree was full of huge green leaves bigger than Matt's hands, which turned to shades of bright orange and crimson in the fall. Matt used to climb that tree often to tease Attila, hiding from him among those humongous leaves.

Now they were moving to an apartment where he would share a bedroom with his brother. They wouldn't even have a yard, only a small balcony.

Many of his friends' families had already left his Boston neighborhood. About one-third of the houses on his block were empty. Some of the families had to give up their houses because the parents lost their jobs. But many others, like Matt's family, simply couldn't afford to keep paying for their houses.

Matt's dad had tried to explain it around the dinner table one night.

"I made a mistake," he told them simply.

He said that they had borrowed money on their house with something called a 2/28 mortgage, but when he had done it, he hadn't fully understood how the mortgage worked. Unlike their old mortgage, the loan payments on this mortgage had gone up suddenly, and Matt's parents didn't make enough money to afford those higher payments. They were several months behind on the loan, and the man who had arranged for the mortgage was telling them that they could no longer keep the house.

"If we don't leave," his dad solemnly told them, "he said the sheriff will come and make us leave."

Matt vaguely remembered a man coming to their house a few years earlier, encouraging his parents to take out a new loan that he called a "refinancing." They were all excited because the man said they would get enough money to replace their leaky roof and have some left over for a nice vacation. They thought this man was trying to help them. His dad took the loan and replaced the roof, but instead of taking a vacation, he put the extra money in a savings account for Matt's college.

But now, his dad told them, "All of our savings are gone."

Matt's college account was gone. Everything. His parents had used it all up trying to make the higher payments so they could keep their house.

Matt had never seen his dad cry, but he did that night. And then things got even worse when they couldn't find a new place to live that would take Attila.

Matt's thoughts were interrupted by his mother calling him to breakfast from the kitchen downstairs. He climbed out of bed and saw Attila struggling to follow. He gently wrapped his arms around the old dog's hindquarters, lifted him to a standing position, and helped him walk to the edge of the bed, where Matt had built a ramp out of sofa cushions. With Matt holding up his hindquarters, the dog shuffled down the cushions onto the floor. Matt pulled on a pair of jeans and a T-shirt and ran his fingers through his hair as Attila patiently waited. Then together they left the bedroom and slowly made their way down the stairs, Attila softly whimpering in pain with each step.

Matt took Attila outside behind the old tool shed where Attila always did his business. Then they found a sunny patch in the backyard and lay down together, Matt on his back, gazing up at the clear sky. He knew this could be the last time the dog would enjoy the coolness of thick grass underneath him and the warmth of the morning sun. Matt winced at the memory of his visit to the shelter with his parents a few weeks earlier to make arrangements for Attila. He had had to fight off tears when he saw the small chain-link pens the dogs lived in, with their hard gray concrete floors.

Matt's mom brought Matt an egg sandwich and sat next to him on the grass while he ate it. Pretty soon Matt's dad and brother joined them in the backyard. They sat in a circle around Attila, simultaneously giving him scratches in all his favorite places: behind his ears, his neck, his tummy, and on his hind end, right above his tail.

"We have to go now," Matt's dad finally said. "Matt, get Attila's dog bed and blanket, and put them in the car."

Matt retrieved Attila's bedding from the corner

of the kitchen where he usually slept and carefully arranged it in the backseat of their minivan. When Matt was finished, his dad picked Attila up and gently laid him in the car. Matt and his brother squeezed in on either side of the dog and petted him all the long way to the shelter. Matt rolled down his window and, with his brother's help, got Attila close enough to the window that the old dog could stick his nose out and feel the wind rushing by.

The shelter's staff were expecting them when they arrived and had already prepared Attila's pen. The family made a little parade back to Attila's new home. A shelter worker led the way, followed by Matt's dad, carrying Attila, Matt with the dog bed and blanket, his mom with Attila's food bowl, and his little brother with some chew toys. They all stood around him in the pen, hugging and kissing him one final time. As they left, the old dog looked confused and struggled to follow them out before the shelter worker closed the gate. Attila looked at Matt through the chain link, questioning, his ears and tail down, as if he thought he had done something wrong. Why was he in this strange, cold place? Why was Matt leaving him? Matt didn't understand either.

The rest of the day the family spent packing and moving all of their stuff to their new two-bedroom apartment. Matt hated the cramped apartment. He hated not having a yard. He hated the extra mile he had to walk to get to school. But most of all, he hated not having Attila.

Every Saturday morning for three months the family made the long drive from their new apartment to the shelter to visit their beloved pet. At each visit they would ask the shelter workers if any families had asked about adopting the old dog. The answer was always no. Then one Saturday the woman who ran the shelter asked to talk with Matt's parents privately.

Matt and his brother took Attila to a small courtyard behind the shelter while their parents met with the woman. Above the courtyard's high concrete walls they could see the tips of trees whose browning leaves broke easily from their branches, slowly fluttering down in the autumn breeze. Attila would perk his ears each time a leaf fell close to him.

Matt's parents soon joined them and suggested that they stay with the dog through lunch. Matt's mom left to get some sandwiches and doggie treats at a nearby grocery store. They picnicked in the courtyard, and Attila proved that he could still count and high-five with his paw when rewarded with one of the treats.

After lunch they took Attila back to his pen and made him comfortable on his bed.

"You should stay with him for a while," Matt's mom said to him. "We'll wait outside by the car for you."

Matt understood what she was telling him. He didn't want to understand, but he did. He stayed for a long time, stroking Attila's back until the old dog drifted off to sleep. Then he kissed him in what he thought would be his second and final good-bye.

They drove back to the apartment in silence. Matt went to the bedroom he shared with his brother and closed the door. He had to be alone.

I can't let it happen, he thought to himself. *There has got to be a way to save him.*

He logged on to his computer and started searching Google. He used the search terms "German shepherd," "help," "needs home," and "please rescue." Finally, he found a website for an organization that said they took in German shepherds who needed homes and that they had a big farm where they kept them, just a few miles away. Matt sent a desperate e-mail to the address listed on the website. He explained the whole situation, about his family losing their house and how the shelter where Attila was staying would soon put him to sleep.

Matt tossed and turned that night, hoping against hope that this organization would help him. He rose early the next morning after hardly sleeping at all.

The first thing he did was turn on his computer to check his e-mail messages. His heart started pounding when he saw a message from the shepherd rescue organization.

"Dear Matt," the e-mail began. "We were deeply moved by your story and the obvious love and devotion you have for your dog. And we are so sorry that your family lost your house. This has been happening all over the country. We have too many dogs now and cannot accept any more. But when one of our volunteers saw your e-mail, she agreed to adopt Attila. Her name is Marsha, and she lives in the country with lots of land. Attila will be quite happy there, and you can visit him any time you want."

The rest of the e-mail provided driving instructions to Marsha's house, and said she would be waiting for him that day. Matt excitedly printed the e-mail, then woke his still-sleeping brother. "GET UP!" he shouted. "We have to go get Attila." He rushed out of the room to give his parents the good news, showing them the e-mail. For the second time in his life, Matt saw his father weep, and he realized how hard losing their house and Attila had been on his dad.

It was Sunday, and Mom insisted that they go to church to give their thanks before driving to the shelter to pick up Attila. She called the shelter to let the staff know they had found a new home for Attila and would be by around noon to pick him up. Matt hardly heard the sermon at all—he was so anxious to rescue Attila from the shelter.

The shelter workers had everything packed up for them when they arrived, and they helped Matt's family carry all of Attila's things out to the car. Attila lay down in his usual place between Matt and his brother in the backseat, sniffing at the air coming through Matt's open window.

They drove for nearly an hour before reaching Marsha's house. As they turned into Marsha's driveway, they saw a beautiful old wood farmhouse surrounded by acres and acres of land. Marsha came out of her house to greet them, then led them into the house and showed them a corner of her kitchen where Attila would be sleeping. Matt carefully arranged Attila's bed, blanket, bowl, and toys there. They spent the rest of the afternoon with Marsha, sitting under an old maple tree in her front yard, telling her stories about Attila, the things he liked to do, and how he could still do simple tricks like counting and high fives. She said that he was a very special dog, and that she would take good care of him, and that they should come back and visit as many times as they wanted.

As the sun started to set, they said their good-byes, and Matt gave Attila a very long hug. It wasn't so hard to say good-bye this time, because he knew this farewell would not be his last.

WHY DID MATT'S FAMILY LOSE THEIR HOUSE?

Houses are big investments for most families. They can cost hundreds of thousands of dollars, which is much more than most people make in a year. For that reason, people borrow money to buy their houses and then pay the loan back over a long period of time, usually thirty years.

Where does the money for these loans come from? Most of it used to come from banks who would take some of the money that people deposited into their bank accounts and lend it to other families to buy homes. Banks that specialized in making home loans were called "savings and loans" or "thrift" institutions. Maybe you have seen the movie *It's a Wonderful Life*, when Jimmy Stewart explains to people who are trying to withdraw all of their money from his bank that he doesn't have it all—that most of it has been lent out to their neighbors to buy homes.

This is how it would work: Families and others would deposit their money into the bank. In return the bank or thrift would agree to pay them something called "interest" on their deposits for as long as they left their money at the bank. Interest is usually expressed as a percentage. For instance, a bank might agree to pay a family 5% on their deposits each year, or $5 for every $100 deposited. (Interest rates on deposits are a lot lower than 5% as I write this in 2013, but we will use that number to keep the math easy.) The bank would then take some of that money and lend it to other families to buy houses. The bank would charge those families a higher interest rate—say, 10% (again, interest rates on home loans are lower as I write this, but 10% keeps the math easy). With the interest earned on their loans, the bank could pay depositors their 5% and have another 5% to cover its own expenses and salaries for bank employees. By charging homeowners higher interest rates than it paid depositors on their bank accounts, banks made money.

But there were risks in doing business this way. One risk was that the homeowner might not pay the loan back. In that case, the money would be gone, but the bank would still need to make good on its obligations to depositors. To reduce this risk, banks would require something called a mortgage from homeowners. A mortgage meant that if a homeowner could not pay the loan back, the family would have to give up their house to the bank, which could then sell it to someone else to get its money back.

But taking someone's house from them was an expensive and unpleasant process. Bankers making mortgage loans usually knew the families who borrowed from them. They might have kids going to school together, or they might belong to the same clubs. It was bad for a bank's reputation to take a house away from someone in their community. And even when they had to take back the house, banks couldn't always sell it for the full amount of the loan. For that reason, banks were usually very careful about making home loans and took steps to make sure the borrower had enough income to pay the loan back. Banks were so careful, in fact, that prior to 2007, less than 2% of all homeowners failed to repay their home loans.

SECURITIZATION: SOLVING ONE PROBLEM, CREATING ANOTHER

When mortgages were made by banks lending out their deposits, the percentage of borrowers who defaulted on their mortgages stayed low. That is because banks were scrupulous about making sure that borrowers could repay them. If the borrowers couldn't repay, the banks had to suffer the losses.

So while this kind of lending worked well to make sure that home buyers got mortgages they could had a problem. But they couldn't. So they started losing money.

This mismatch between interest rates on mortgages that were fixed for 30 years and interest rates on deposits that were always changing led to another financial crisis—called the S&L crisis—because most of the banks that got into trouble were old savings and loan institutions that specialized in mortgage lending. Though that crisis wasn't as bad as the 2008 one in its impact on our economy, it cost the government a lot of money and caused bank managers and regulators to look for ways to make sure it didn't happen again. Securitization was meant to solve the problem. Once mortgages were made, instead of banks holding on to them, they would be pooled into securitizations and sold off to investors—investors like pension funds, life insurance companies, even retired people—who were happy to receive the same rate on their investment for many, many years. Banks could take the money they made by selling the loans into securitizations to make new loans at whatever interest rate was prevailing at the time.

This worked for a while, particularly when most mortgages were being originated by regulated banks and sold to government-created companies called Fannie Mae and Freddie Mac, which guaranteed the afford, it created another kind of problem called a "duration mismatch." You know what a mismatch is. If you play a soccer game against another school and lose 7 to 0, your teams were probably mismatched in their skills and abilities. If your three-year-old brother puts on your mom's high heels, his feet will be mismatched with her shoes (among other mismatches). Well, 30-year, fixed-rate loans didn't match up very well with bank deposits. The problem was that the interest rate on those loans was fixed for 30 years, but the interest rate on deposits changed all the time.

In the 1970s, mortgage interest rates were around 8% to 10%, while the interest rates banks had to pay on deposits were more like 5% to 7%. This generally meant that the interest that banks received on their loans was about 3% higher than the amount they had to pay out on their deposits. However, in the late 1970s, interest rates on deposit accounts skyrocketed, reaching 16% in the early 1980s. That meant that all of a sudden, banks were having to pay much higher rates on their deposits than they were receiving on the 30-year loans they had made in previous years. If the banks had been able to lock in deposit rates for 30 years, the way home buyers could lock in the interest they paid on their mortgages, banks wouldn't have payments on the mortgage-backed securities. (More about Fannie and Freddie in Part 2.) However, it began to break down when big financial institutions started doing the securitizations without keeping any obligation to protect investors against loans defaulting. Once that happened, lending standards started to deteriorate and millions of mortgages were made that people couldn't repay.

Then something called securitization happened, which dramatically changed the way people got home loans. With securitization, big financial institutions would pool together thousands of mortgages and put them into something called a trust. Investors—usually other big financial institutions like pension funds, insurance companies, and mutual funds—would pay for pieces of these trusts, which gave them the right to receive some of the loan payments. These pieces were called "mortgage-backed securities." Because of securitization, money for the mortgages didn't have to come from banks lending their deposits anymore. So lots of people got into the business of making mortgages.

Here are the basic steps in a mortgage securitization:

1) A person called a "mortgage originator" agrees to make a mortgage loan to Matt's family.

2) The mortgage originator contacts a "securitizer"—usually a big bank or other financial firm—and lets it know that he has a mortgage to sell.

3) The securitizer, oftentimes working with a big bank, provides funds to the originator to make the mortgage, then puts it in a pool with other mortgages.

4) The loan payments on that and thousands of other mortgages in the pool are divided up into pieces called mortgage-backed securities and sold to other big institutions.

5) The securitizer uses that money to buy more pools of loans.

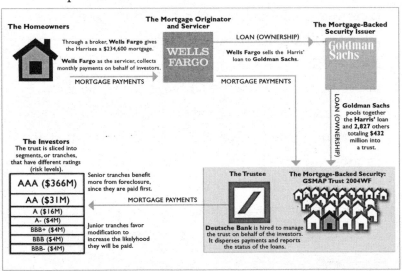

Securitization had some benefits. For one thing, it made more money available for mortgages so more people could buy homes. But it also created several problems. First, a lot of people who were not banks got into the mortgage-making business. The government heavily regulates banks that take deposits, and that is a good thing. A mortgage is a huge obligation for most families, and they should be borrowing money from responsible lenders who are overseen by the government. But with securitization, just about anybody could make a mortgage. A lot of these people weren't really well trained, and there was no government agency watching them to make sure families were getting mortgages they could repay.

But even more importantly, the people arranging the mortgages didn't have a reason to care if the borrowers could pay the loan back because they were just passing them on to big securitizers who were, in turn, selling interests in the loan payments to other big institutions. These "mortgage originators," like the one that visited Matt's family, were paid generous fees for arranging these mortgages up front. They figured out quickly, the more loans they made, the more they got paid, so they started originating as many as possible, without regard to whether people could pay them back. They didn't have community ties in the same way as a traditional bank. And the big financial institutions who securitized and bought the "pieces" of these mortgage pools didn't know the borrowers at all, so they didn't feel the same commitment to them that a traditional bank might have.

Greed overtook the process, and mortgage originators started getting the idea that it was actually a good thing to make loans to people who couldn't repay them, because that would force them to get another loan to pay off the unaffordable one. When a homeowner takes out a new loan to pay off the old one, it is called "refinancing." These greedy originators started actively looking for people who were on tight budgets or people who were known to have had trouble in the past with managing their money. These people were called "subprime borrowers." But they also targeted other vulnerable families, like Matt's parents, who had responsibly managed their finances but were not sophisticated when it came to financial matters and had an immediate need for cash. Sometimes they would target entire neighborhoods, as was the case in the area where Matt lived. Boston was one of many cities throughout the country where unscrupulous mortgage originators targeted neighborhoods.

Most of the subprime borrowers, like Matt's family, already owned homes and had mortgages with payments that they could afford and were fixed at the same amount over the entire 30-year life of the loan. Many middle- and low-income families had received their mortgages through a program run by a government agency called the Federal Housing Administration, or FHA. These were safe, affordable mortgages, but mortgage originators would actively seek these families out and convince them to take out new loans called "2/28s" and "3/27s." Indeed, loans arranged through the FHA declined from 14% of all home purchases in 2001 to 3% by 2005. These families refinanced into loans being securitized by big financial institutions.

Most of these loans did not have fixed payments. Rather, after two or three years the payments on them would shoot up dramatically, usually to unaffordable levels, and could keep going up over the remaining years of the loan. This is why they were called 2/28s and 3/27s, because the payment was lower for the first 2 or 3 years, then shot up over the remaining 28 years (for a 2/28) or 27 years (for a 3/27) of the loan. To escape the higher payment, the homeowners would have to go back to the mortgage originator to get a new loan to pay off the old one, and that new loan would once again have a steep payment increase after a few years. Each time a family refinanced—that is, got a new loan to pay off the old one—the mortgage originator would get more money. The new loan would always be bigger than the old one to provide some extra cash to pay the mortgage originator and sometimes give the families something extra too—in Matt's case, money to replace the roof.

This only worked so long as the family's home was worth more than the amount of the new mortgage. If home prices kept going up, securitizers and the investors who bought mortgage-backed securities thought that it was okay to keep making bigger and bigger loans to subprime families. They figured that if the family stopped paying the mortgage, securitizers could just claim the house and sell it to get their money back. But home prices didn't keep going up. They doubled from 2001 to 2006, but in late 2006 they started to decline. Now securitizers had a problem. They had made all of these big loans to borrowers whose houses were no longer worth more than the amount of the loan, and they didn't want to lend them any more money. As a result, families like Matt's who had mortgages with big payment increases could no longer get new loans to pay off the old ones. This is one of the reasons why so many people could no longer afford their mortgages and ended up losing their homes.

And the payment increases could be huge. Let's say a family borrowed $150,000 on their house. A typical subprime loan in 2006 charged an interest rate of 9%, which would jump to 13% after two to three years. This worked out to a monthly payment of about $1,200 during the first few years, jumping to $1,650 after that. For families like Matt's, who were already on a tight budget, they simply couldn't keep up the payments. So the securitizer started a "foreclosure," a legal process to take their homes away from them.

As of August 2013 about 6.75 million homes had been lost to foreclosure or sold by families facing foreclosure since the beginning of 2007. There were an additional million homes in the process of foreclosure, and another 2.1 million that were expected to enter foreclosure because the homeowners had not made mortgage payments for many months. About 10 million families are likely to lose their homes in the aftermath of the financial crisis. This represents about one in every five homeowners.

Having to give up their pets has been just one of the many bad consequences for these millions of families who have lost their homes. In Matt's hometown of Boston, for instance, animal shelters reported a big jump in people giving up their pets because of financial reasons, including losing their homes to foreclosure. This put a real strain on animal shelters throughout the country. Most animal shelters are supported by donations, and as people were hurt by the financial crisis, they couldn't afford to be as generous as they were in the past. So animal shelters were receiving less money to support their operations, even as more and more families were bringing their pets to them.

CHAPTER 2

ANNA

They were moving again. Anna couldn't believe it. They had moved three times in the last three years. She still had boxes in her bedroom from their last move, which she hadn't yet unpacked.

She didn't understand why her dad kept moving the family. For the first ten years of her life, they lived in a nice two-story house on a street called Elms' Way, named for the huge elms that lined the street and shaded the entire neighborhood. The house belonged to her grandmother, who lived with them until she passed away three years ago. The house was painted white, with green trim and shutters. It had a spacious basement with knotty-wood paneling and an apple-green linoleum floor. The basement was so big that

Anna was able to ride her tricycle around and around in it when she was a toddler. When she got older, she and her friends would use the basement to have sleepovers. They would dance on the linoleum floor to tunes on their iPods. Or they would pop popcorn and sip sodas while watching movies on the wide-screen TV that stood in the corner, then stay up all night talking. The house also had a large backyard, where Anna and her field hockey team could practice in the off-season.

When Grandma died, Dad decided to sell the house because he said they could make a lot of money off it.

"Home prices are so hot," she remembered him saying. "Everybody wants to live in Southern California, and they will pay lots of money to live here."

So Anna's dad sold Grandma's house and bought a much bigger one that had a swimming pool in the backyard. Instead of using the money they received from selling Grandma's house to buy the new one, her dad borrowed a lot of money to pay for it.

"This way we have money to buy a new car and take a vacation to Europe," he said.

They spent almost a whole summer in Europe staying at fancy hotels, then returned home to their fancy new house. Anna liked the new house at first. It was more modern than Grandma's house, with flat-screen TVs in almost every room. She had her own bathroom, one that she didn't have to share with anyone else. But it was a long way from town and her school, and all the other houses in the neighborhood were really far apart. She missed her old neighborhood, where the houses were close together and all the kids could run in a pack to each other's houses. There weren't many kids in her new neighborhood, and their houses were too far away to reach by foot.

Not that it mattered much, because after six months her dad decided to sell that house for another one. This one was even bigger. It had a horse stable (but no horses) and a tennis court. But it was so far out in the country, it took her mom an hour each way to take her to and from school. There were no kids out there at all and no houses for miles around. The house needed a lot of work. The roof leaked in places, and the plumbing made terrible, scary noises—like ghosts in an old horror movie—whenever you flushed the upstairs toilets. Her dad hired some men to come over and fix the roof, and to repair and repaint the ceilings so no one could see the water stains. Then he put that house up for sale and sold it after several months. He bragged that he had sold the house for $100,000 more than he had paid for it.

Her mom wanted to use that money to buy a house back in their old neighborhood.

But Dad said, "Houses are still hot. This time I am

going to borrow money to buy two houses, one where we will live and one to sell right away."

So they moved again, this time into a house on a golf course (though her parents didn't play golf), which stood in a neighborhood that was surrounded by a huge ten-foot-high black iron fence. Most of the people who lived there were much older than Anna's parents, and there were no kids at all. Anna's family couldn't even drive to their own house without stopping and checking in with a guard who sat in a little house at the main gate. The golf course was pretty and all the houses in the neighborhood were brand-new, but only about half of them had people living in them. The rest had FOR SALE signs in their front yards.

The other house Dad bought was just down the street from the one they lived in. Anna didn't understand why, but he told her and her mom that they had to put some of their furniture and clothes and things into that house so it would look like they were living there too. Every other week or so, they would go over to that house and spend the night. Her dad brought a lot of people over to look at the house to see if they wanted to buy it. Whenever he did, Anna and her mom would have to go over there and tell them how much they enjoyed living there. Anna hated lying. It didn't feel right.

But no one seemed to want to buy that house, even though her dad kept lowering the price. Anna could hear her dad and mom arguing at night when they thought she was asleep. Her mom was angry because they didn't have enough money to make payments on the loans they had taken to buy the two houses. Her dad had quit his job as a realtor when he started making so much money buying and selling houses. But no one wanted to buy houses anymore, and Anna's parents were stuck. Mom was working part-time as a receptionist at a doctor's office, but that wasn't nearly enough to support them. Dad had tried to get his job back, but business was bad at the real estate company where he used to work, and they weren't hiring people.

Lots of angry people started calling the house. Anna's parents told her not to answer the phone. Anna was miserable listening to the phone ring and ring, especially when she thought it might be a friend calling. But more often than not, it was someone calling to leave an "urgent" message on their answering machine, telling her mom and dad that they needed to call back right away or face "legal action." At first it was people calling about the money her parents owed on the houses, but after a while others started calling too—the electric company, the company that picked up their trash, the cable TV company, and others.

Finally, a man came to their house one night and told Anna's parents that he would give them $10,000 if they vacated both houses and gave him the keys. Dad agreed, and they all sat down at the kitchen table. Dad started signing a bunch of papers while Anna's mom sobbed softly. When they were finished, the man told Anna's dad that they had thirty days to leave the houses.

So now they were moving again, but not to a new house. They were packing up their car and moving to Kansas City to live with Aunt Karen, Anna's mom's sister, while Anna's dad tried to find work. Anna had always lived near the ocean, and she tried to imagine living in a place that was surrounded with nothing but land. Her mom said that there were lots of wheat fields around Kansas City that looked a little like ocean waves when the wind blew. She said the economy was much better there and Dad could probably find a decent job, but it would be a long time before they could buy a house again.

They drove for three days before reaching her aunt's house. It was a pretty two-story house, sitting on another treelined street. Anna was happy to see two girls her age practicing field hockey in front of the house next door. Aunt Karen, her husband, Tom, and their eight-year-old son, Harry, all came outside to greet Anna and her family as they pulled into the driveway.

"I've made cinnamon bread," said Aunt Karen. "Mom's old recipe." Anna could smell the aroma of cinnamon and nutmeg as they entered the house, and it brought back such good memories of their house on Elms' Way, with its roomy kitchen where her grandmother would bake bread, cookies, and other savory things. Aunt Karen took them down to the basement to show them where they would be staying. The basement was clean and cozy, with two bedrooms, a small kitchen, and a full bathroom. Best of all, it had knotty-pine walls and a green linoleum tile floor. There was nothing fancy about it—no swimming pools or horse stables here. But Anna felt like she was finally back home.

WHY DID ANNA'S FAMILY LOSE THEIR HOUSE?

Matt's family lost their house because they had a subprime mortgage that had big payment increases they could not afford. Their mistake was in getting a mortgage that seemed affordable based on the payments during the first few years, but became unaffordable later on. They were taken advantage of by a mortgage originator who pretended to have their interests at heart but was really only interested in getting money for himself.

Anna's dad, on the other hand, was more sophisticated and thought he knew what he was doing. He his payment could more than double. But he had no intention of making payments for more than five years. His goal was to quickly sell, or "flip" the house, in a matter of months.

And why was Anna's dad even able to get a loan when he didn't have a job? That was because he took out something called a "NINJA." These loans had nothing to do with teenage mutant turtles. This kind of "NINJA" stands for no-income, no-job, no-assets. Again, because mortgage originators were so eager to make as many loans as they could, they started making loans to people who couldn't even prove they had income. Instead, the originator would fill out false paperwork making it look like borrowers had income when they really didn't. The securitizer also wouldn't bother to verify whether the paperwork was correct. By 2006 it is estimated that 84% of pick-a-pay mortgages were made without good proof of income. Anna's dad may have known that the originator who arranged for his loans gave false information to the securitizer about his income, but in many situations the borrowers didn't even know that originators were lying about their income.

Why did Anna's dad make her pretend like she was living in the other house on the golf course? That was because it was much easier to get a loan if you lived in understood a lot about buying and selling houses as a professional realtor. He knew that home prices were going up rapidly and that through the process of securitization, it was easy to get loans to buy and sell houses to make a profit. So instead of buying a house to provide a comfortable, safe place for his family to live, where Anna could be close to her school and friends, he moved the family around a lot to make money. No doubt Anna's dad thought he was doing the best thing for his family. But he failed to see how painful it was for Anna to keep moving. And by quitting his job, he left his family vulnerable. He thought home prices would just keep going up forever, so he could keep making money buying them at one price and selling them for a higher price. But home prices couldn't go up forever.

Anna's dad knew a lot about mortgages as well. So he stayed away from the expensive subprime loans that proved to be so devastating for Matt's family. Instead, he took out mortgages called "option ARM" or "pick-a-pays." These loans basically let sophisticated borrowers make very small mortgage payments during the first five years of the loan, then make much bigger "catch-up payments" later. With a "pick-a-pay," Anna's dad would have a monthly payment that was about half of what Matt's dad paid on his subprime loan. Of course, if Anna's dad had kept the loan for more than five years, the house you were buying. Investors in securitizations thought it was less likely that you would default on your mortgage if you were buying a house as your home. So if your house was what they called "owner-occupied," it was easier to get a mortgage than if you were buying a house simply to try to resell it later and make money off it. This is why Anna's dad lied and said they were living in both houses so he could get cheaper loans on both houses, but he had to keep up appearances so he wouldn't get caught.

Anna's dad got into trouble when home prices started going down and fewer people wanted to buy houses. Think about it. Would you want to buy a house for $150,000 when in a year it might be worth only $125,000? That is what happens when home prices start going down. People stop buying because they figure that if they wait a year or two, they can get a cheaper price. It's like waiting to buy a bike or computer game until it goes on sale.

The other problem was that too many houses were built in Southern California and a lot of other parts of the country. This is what is called "oversupply." Just like Anna's dad, home builders got all excited about making lots of money building and selling houses as home prices kept rising. They built more houses than there were families who wanted to buy them. They also built houses that were too expensive and that were in inconvenient locations, thinking that the housing craze would go on forever, and that people would buy anything. But this started to change in 2006, which is why there were so many FOR SALE signs in the remote golf-course neighborhood where Anna's dad bought those two houses.

Matt's parents voluntarily gave up their house to the mortgage company representing the securitizer, not wanting to go through the embarrassment of having it taken away from them. Being a realtor, Anna's dad knew that the legal costs of foreclosure could be quite substantial and that many mortgage companies were willing to pay families to give up their homes to avoid those legal costs. This is called "cash for keys," and it is why the mortgage company gave Anna's dad $10,000. This was money that would help them move and establish a new life in Kansas City.

THE LAW OF SUPPLY AND DEMAND

Nothing is more basic to the understanding of how economies and markets work than the law of supply and demand.

But it isn't really a "law." It is just a common-sense understanding of how people think and act when buying and selling things.

For instance, when more people want something—and supply stays the same—the price will go up. That is because the people selling that something will realize that they can charge more for it, the more people want to buy it. The greater the demand for something, the higher the price, all other things being equal. That is why priceless works of art, like Da Vinci's *Mona Lisa*, have almost infinite value, because there are millions of people who would like to own it for themselves, but only one *Mona Lisa*.

On the other hand, the sculpture I just made while doodling at my desk here, made of a Diet Coke can and paper clips, probably has zero value. Only one of them exists, but nobody besides me wants it (and I'm not even sure that I do) . . .

So the price of something is directly related to how many people want to buy it, and how many of that thing there are to sell. The more demand, the higher the price. On the other hand, the more the supply, the lower the price. If instead of one *Mona Lisa*, Da Vinci had managed to paint 10 million of them, the value of those artworks would be considerably less.

Here is something else that is interesting about supply and demand. When the price of something goes up, supply will eventually go up too. That is because people will see other producers of that thing making lots of money. They will want to make money too, so they will start producing and selling something similar. It will usually take some time for other producers to get their goods or services to market, which will keep prices higher. But once the amount of supply increases, it will bring prices down. (Of course, if, like the *Mona Lisa*, the thing is unique and the supplier is dead, supply will never increase and the price will remain high.)

This interplay between supply and demand will eventually sort out what economists call "equilibrium." That is the point at which the price and quantity of a thing fully reflects the willingness and ability of consumers to pay for it and producers to supply it. In a properly functioning market the equilibrium price of that good or service will be just above the cost of producing one more of it. In general, producers will not want to charge a price that is less than their cost of producing it. If they do that, they will lose money!

BUBBLE, BUBBLE, TOIL AND TROUBLE

"Bubbles" build when the increasing demand for something drives up prices to levels that are not sustainable. With the housing crisis, as with many past bubbles, unsustainable prices occurred when increased demand was largely driven by people borrowing more than they could afford. The problem was made a lot worse when people wanted to buy houses not because they wanted to use them, but because they thought lots of other people wanted them, so they expected the price to go up. Matt's parents bought their house because they wanted a place to live. That's what houses are for: to provide shelter. The value of a house as shelter is what economists call its "intrinsic" value. Anna's dad, on the other hand, wasn't really interested in buying houses to provide good places for his family to live. In fact, he was buying crazy places that were too big for the family and really far away from Anna's school. He bought all those houses because he thought their prices would go up. Buying a thing not because you really want to use it, but because you think the price is going to go up, is called "speculation."

Speculators usually borrow heavily to buy things because, like Anna's dad, they think they will be able to pay off the loan by quickly reselling the thing for a profit. And if they borrow to buy the thing to begin with, then they can buy more of it and make even bigger profits.

For instance, let's say Anna's dad wanted to buy a house for $200,000, and he thought he could resell it in a year for $220,000, to make a $20,000 profit. Let's also say that he could have used the cash he received from selling Anna's grandma's house to buy the new house without borrowing. So he would spend $200,000, and his profit after a year would be $20,000, or a 10% profit.

Now let's say that instead of spending $200,000, he decides he only wants to spend $2,000 of his own money, and he will borrow the rest to buy the house. Let's also say that the interest payments on his mortgage are $12,000 during the first year of his loan. House prices go up as he expects, and he sells the house for $220,000 after a year. He pays the mortgage company $210,000 (the $198,000 loan plus $12,000 interest). He keeps the remaining $10,000 for a profit of $8,000 ($10,000 minus the $2,000 he invested of his own money). The $8,000 he makes is less than the $20,000 he made when he paid for the house all with his own money. But in this example he only put up $2,000 of his own money, so his profit as a percentage of his original investment is a whopping 400%. Of course, if the value of the home declined by 10%, or $20,000 on his $2,000 investment, his loss (the $20,000 plus the $12,000 interest payment) on his original investment would be four times higher—1600%!

By borrowing to speculate, also called using "leverage," speculators can buy a lot more property than they could if they pay cash. In this example, with his $200,000, Anna's dad could have theoretically bought up to 100 houses if all he had to invest of his own money was $2,000 for each house! In fact, during the years leading up to the housing crisis, originators were hardly requiring borrowers to put any of their own money down to buy houses. They could borrow almost the entire purchase price. (Of course, when home prices started to decline, their losses were catastrophic.) With securitization, it became very easy to borrow money, so professional real estate speculators started buying several houses at the same time, which drove up demand for houses, which then drove up prices to unsustainable levels.

Another problem that contributed to this bubble was the failure of loan originators to document borrowers' incomes. In a healthy economy home prices are determined, in part, by how much individuals and families are willing to pay for homes, which, in turn, is based on how much money they are likely to earn over the course of the loan. Before the housing craziness, bankers usually required home buyers to have enough income so that their mortgage payment did not exceed more than 35% of their monthly income. Based on past experience, they knew that if the mortgage payment took a bigger percentage of a family's income, the family could have trouble paying it back. So for instance, if a family made $5,000 a month, the mortgage payment could not exceed $1,750 (35% of $5,000). Requiring that homeowners provide proof of their income, and allowing them to buy only houses that they could reasonably afford based on that income, had the effect of limiting home price increases. Home prices could only go up if homeowners could afford to pay more based on rising incomes. Basing loan decisions on documented income levels and how much a family could reasonably afford to spend helped ensure that when home prices went up, those home prices were more in line with what people could afford to pay on a home loan.

When loan originators stopped making loans based on what families could afford, this increased demand, pushing up prices. This is because lots of families who would not have been able to qualify for a loan under the old, tougher lending standards could now get one. In fact, during the years 2000–2006, home prices nearly doubled. For a time, home prices were rising twice as fast as people's incomes. And for middle- and lower-income families, their real income was actually declining even as home prices kept going up and up.

From 2000–2006, Houses Became
A Lot More Expensive

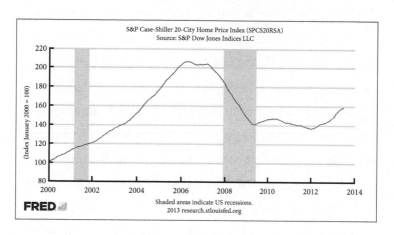

While People Were Making Less Money

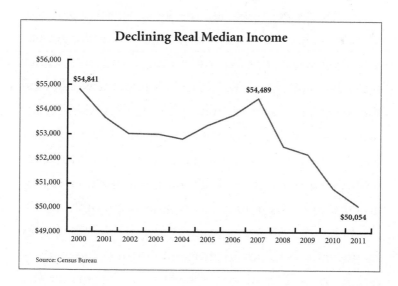

Builders were rushing to keep up with all of that increased demand by building a lot more houses. But the increased demand wasn't all coming from people who actually wanted to live in those houses. Many were just speculating. And as prices went up, people who really did want to buy houses to live in found it harder and harder to find one that they could afford, and demand for houses started to go down. With fewer buyers, and many speculators wanting to sell, prices stopped rising and then began to fall. Instead of a market where everyone expected home prices to go up, everyone suddenly expected home prices to fall. Speculators and others rushed to sell before prices fell further. Buyers held back, not wanting to buy a house that would lose value.

As prices began to fall, the loose lending practices became a big problem. Speculators could no longer pay off their loans by reselling their houses for a profit. They started defaulting on their loans, and no one would lend them any more money. What's more, they didn't really care about walking away from their loans because they had hardly invested any of their own money to begin with. Also, they frequently didn't live in the houses they bought, so it was no big deal to give them up.

When speculators could no longer borrow money to buy houses, demand dropped further, and with it, home prices. The supply of homes on the market also increased as mortgage companies took their houses and tried to sell them to others to get some of their money back. People like Matt's family, who had mortgages with big payment increases they could not afford, also lost their homes because they could no longer refinance, and these homes were put up for sale, adding to the excess supply. With both supply increasing and demand dropping, home prices fell sharply. They dropped by over 30% from 2006 to 2009 and did not really start to rise again until 2012. In other words, if a house was worth $100,000 in 2006 and its value dropped by the average percentage, it was worth only $70,000 by 2009.

CHAPTER 3

JORGE

It was cold standing on the train platform.
Jorge stomped his feet to stay warm, wishing that he
was wearing winter boots instead of nylon sneakers.
His feet had grown two sizes since last winter, but
he knew there was no money for warm boots. The
sneakers would be his only shoes for some time.

Jorge looked over at his big brother, who didn't
seem to be bothered by the cold at all. José looked
so impressive in his Marine khakis and lace-up black
books. When their dad lost his job, José lost his dream
of going to college. There was no money for that, and
José didn't want to be another mouth to feed with Dad
out of work. So he had enlisted in the Marines, and
now they were shipping him out to Afghanistan. This

would be the last time they would see him for at least six months.

Jorge, his dad, and José turned their heads in unison as they heard the whistle of the coming train. Jorge wanted to be grown-up, but he couldn't hold back the tears, realizing that his brother would soon be on his way to a war-ravaged country halfway across the world, where a bullet could kill him, or a land mine could send him home without a leg or an arm. José was so brave to face that kind of danger; Jorge was humiliated that he couldn't control his tears. José bent over him and gave him a reassuring hug.

"The cold makes your eyes water, doesn't it?" José asked him, smiling. "Now, you help Dad take care of your two little sisters. If you don't help out at home, I'm going to hear about it and come back and whup your behind."

Jorge wiped his eyes and managed a smile, and gave a soft punch to José's chest. José rubbed his knuckles on the top of Jorge's head, then turned to their dad and gave him a big bear hug. Jorge's dad was about four inches shorter than his oldest son. He seemed even smaller now, standing next to José, who was so imposing in his Marine camouflage and cap. As the train pulled into the station, José boarded right away. Jorge saw that the cold was bothering José's eyes too.

Jorge and his dad stood on the platform in silence for several minutes after the train left the station. Then Jorge's dad said simply, "Let's go." They headed back to the car to go home.

Jorge's four-year-old twin sisters were waiting for them at their house with his aunt Isabella, his father's sister, who had been helping out ever since his mom had left. Mom had stuck around for a while after Dad lost his job at the cable company. He had worked there for twenty years and was paid nearly $6,000 a month. But business was bad at the cable company. Lots of people in Cleveland were losing their jobs and their homes, just like Jorge's family. They couldn't pay for luxuries like cable TV. So the company started letting people go, including Jorge's dad.

Dad struggled to find work. He started doing odd jobs, painting houses, anything that would pay. But he was barely making $2,000 a month, and the loan payments on their house alone were $3,000 a month, plus all the other expenses they had to pay for their electricity, water, and phone. They had lived in their house for nearly fifteen years, and had fifteen years left on their mortgage. But Jorge's dad just couldn't keep up with the mortgage payments, and he was terrified that they would lose their house after making payments all of those years.

Jorge's dad became sad and irritable. He had always

been a proud man. He liked the fact that he supported his family and paid all of his bills on time. He called Jorge's mom his "little *enamorada*" which meant, "love" in Spanish. He was always bringing her gifts, like flowers and candy. He refused to let her get a job, even as they were falling behind on their bills. They would fight angrily at night, after Jorge and his sisters went to bed. She would say that he needed to call the bank and tell them that they needed help on their mortgage. But he was too proud to ask for help from anyone. "I can handle this. It's okay," he would say. But it wasn't.

Then one morning Jorge's mom announced at the breakfast table that she was leaving that day.

"I'm sorry," she told us. "I can't take it anymore. I can't live like this." Dad didn't say a word. He quietly turned and walked out of the house. José just looked sad. "Mom, don't do this," he said, but she held her hand up and said, "I'm leaving." And she was gone.

Things got worse after that. One of the twins fell on the playground at school and broke her arm and hurt her back. When Dad had worked at the cable company, they had given him health insurance to pay for things like doctor's bills, but he had lost that when they let him go. The school called an ambulance, which took his sister to the emergency room at the hospital, and all the bills from the hospital and doctors added up to

$12,000. Dad had to use a lot of his savings to pay the medical bills. He had saved $50,000 while he worked at the cable company. He was hoping to use some of that money to pay for Jorge to go to college. But what he didn't spend on medical bills, he ended up spending to try to keep the house. He kept hoping he would find a better job, but nothing turned up.

Finally, José found out about a group of people who helped families in financial trouble to get reductions in their mortgage payments. They contacted the bank that had given Jorge's family the loan, and they were able to negotiate a new loan payment of $1,400 a month. With that reduction the family was able to afford the mortgage payments and keep the house. At first Jorge's dad was angry that José had gone behind his back to get help, but he was also relieved that they were going to be able to keep their house.

The cable company eventually hired Dad back part-time. And he kept doing odd jobs too. José sent them part of his Marine pay, and slowly Dad was able to start saving some money. The next winter they had enough to buy Jorge snow boots, and the twins new warm parkas. In the spring their mom returned, but only on the condition that she would work part-time at a dress shop. They still struggled to make ends meet, but the family was back together again.

WHY DID JORGE'S DAD LOSE HIS JOB?

Matt's and Anna's families lost their homes because they took out mortgages they couldn't afford based on their income. With Matt's family, they were misled into thinking the mortgage was affordable when it wasn't. With Anna's family, her dad knew he didn't have any income to pay his mortgages, but thought that he could keep paying off his loans by selling his houses for more than he paid for them.

But Jorge's dad's mortgage was affordable when he got it fifteen years before. There was nothing wrong with his original mortgage. He could no longer afford it because he lost his job. He didn't work for anyone who had anything to do with mortgages or buying and selling houses. Yet he ran into trouble, even though he had nothing to do with the housing craziness.

How do people get jobs? And why do they lose them? There are lots of things that determine how many jobs are available for people like Jorge's dad, who need and want to work.

In a healthy economy, businesses produce lots of goods and services that people want to buy. The money that businesses make from producing and selling those goods and services is used to pay wages to the people who work for them. With ample wages those people can, in turn, buy more goods and services. In this way, an economy grows. It is what economists call a "virtuous circle."

But for businesses to thrive and grow, they need to be able to borrow money, just like people who want to buy homes usually need to borrow to pay for them. Starting, running, or expanding a business can be very expensive, just like buying a house. Most people do not have enough money on their own to build a business, so they need to borrow. For small and medium-size businesses, banks usually do most of the lending, and it's important for small businesses to be able to borrow, because that is where most jobs are created. Indeed, small businesses account for 64% of new jobs in the US. Big businesses need to borrow too, but because they are big and established, it is usually easier for them to get loans than for smaller businesses.

When home prices started going up so rapidly from 2000 to 2006, a lot of families and businesses started borrowing money using something called "home equity." Let's say that you bought a house for $100,000, and over the course of three years its estimated value went up to $150,000. In other words, houses similar to yours in the area where you lived were selling for about $150,000. Let's also say that you still owed $80,000 on the loan you took out to buy your house. The difference between the $80,000 still owed on the house and its $150,000 value is called "equity." In this example the home's equity is $70,000. A mortgage originator would arrange a new mortgage for you of, say, $130,000, because, as discussed earlier, mortgage investors were willing to back bigger and bigger mortgage loans as home prices went up. Now you could use that $130,000 to pay off the remaining $80,000 on your old loan. You would have to pay fees of, say, $5,000 to the mortgage originator, but that would still give you $45,000 of cash to spend.

Lots of people did these kinds of "cash-out" refinancings, getting money to buy lots of things like cars, computers, furniture, and appliances, and that spending helped the economy. Many owners of small businesses also used these kinds of refinancings on their homes to operate and grow their businesses, which created jobs. But when home prices started to fall, this source of spending evaporated. In fact, from the beginning of 2006 to the beginning of 2009, American families lost over $8 trillion in home equity. Poof. It was gone. Families and businesses could no longer use increases in the value of their homes for cash to spend money. Not only that, but one out of every four homeowners were saddled with huge debt obligations on their homes—debt that exceeded what their homes were really worth. So, a lot of families and businesses found that they no longer had an easy source of cash from their homes, and that they were also saddled with big mortgage payments on their houses. What did they do? They stopped spending. And companies who sold the things that they used to buy suffered as well. In particular, people stopped buying things that were not necessities—like cable TV service, for instance. That is why the cable company Jorge's dad worked for had to let him go.

But families and businesses were not the only ones who had borrowed too much. Big financial institutions had borrowed too much as well. And they had taken that borrowed money and invested in mortgage-backed securities and things called "derivatives," which made or lost money depending on whether people paid their mortgages. As more and more people stopped making payments on their mortgages, those securities and derivatives started losing money, even though these big financial institutions still had their own debt obligations to pay.

To make matters worse, these derivatives were what are called "synthetic" instruments. With basic mortgage-backed securities, financial institutions actually owned pieces of real mortgages. But with derivatives, it was a world of make-believe. These derivatives were basically ways for financial institutions to bet on whether people would pay their mortgages, the way you might bet on who wins a soccer game. There was no limit on how many bets big financial institutions could place on whether people paid their mortgages. So tens of trillions of dollars of bets were made. This meant that hundreds of billions of losses on mortgages turned into trillions of dollars of losses on derivatives.

As big financial institutions started experiencing losses on their securities and derivatives that were tied to mortgages, nobody wanted to lend them money anymore. As discussed in more detail in later chapters, not only had big institutions borrowed too much money to make bad investments, but they had also borrowed on a very short-term basis. That is, they would borrow using loans that would last only a day, a week, or a few months, which meant that as those short-term loans expired, they would have to take out new loans. Most of the big financial institutions were borrowing from one another, and as losses mounted on their securities and derivatives, they just refused to keep lending to one another. Since they had very little of their own money to support their operations (called capital), they had to stop lending to households and businesses. All of a sudden, even the strongest and healthiest of businesses found it extremely difficult to borrow money.

For instance, businesses routinely use something

called a "credit line" with a bank to make sure they always have enough cash to maintain their operations. Sometimes there is a gap between the time a company makes and sells a product or service and the time it is paid for. For example, perhaps you've run a lemonade stand or helped with a school cookie sale. You have to pay for the ingredients first to make the lemonade or cookies and then you are paid back later, once you sell them. Your parents probably gave you the money to make your lemonade or cookies, but businesses will typically borrow from a bank to help cover the gap between when they make a good and when they sell it. These kinds of loans are called credit lines.

But in 2008 and 2009, as many banks started getting into trouble with their mortgage investments, these credit lines were reduced by about $2.4 trillion. Think of that. There was $2.4 trillion available for US businesses to borrow that went away. Some of these credit lines were also used by households. You may have seen your parents using a credit card. Credit cards are a form of credit line offered by banks. Businesses use credit cards, but families do too, to buy everyday necessities like groceries and clothing. Sometimes families need to use a credit card because they are a bit short of cash. Sometimes they use their credit card because they view it as more convenient than carrying around lots of cash. But whatever the reason, lots of people buy things with credit cards, and when banks pulled back on their ability to use credit cards to buy things, that also hurt the economy.

Things got so bad that the government finally stepped in and temporarily gave the big banks trillions of dollars so that they could stay in business and keep lending. This government support kept the economy from completely falling apart. Unfortunately, many banks were still afraid to lend and the economy suffered. This made people angry, as the government had helped the banks with trillions of dollars, but the economy still suffered. To make matters worse, some of the top people who worked for these big institutions kept paying themselves huge salaries and bonuses. Fortunately, almost all of the money was paid back, but most people (including me) feel that big financial institutions did not do enough to support the economy after taxpayers risked so much to help them.

Not all banks got into trouble. Some of the big banks did not invest heavily in mortgage securities and derivatives and did not borrow excessively with short-term loans. In addition, most of the medium and smaller-size banks did not invest heavily in high-risk mortgages, and they did a much better job of lending during the Great Recession. Even so, 8.8 million people lost their jobs, and another 4.4 million were forced to work part-time. Though we have made some progress in getting people back to work, by the beginning of 2013, 7.7 million people were still looking for work but couldn't find it. What's worse, a lot of people have given up trying. At the end of 2006, before the financial crisis began, 66.4% of working-age people were either employed or looking for employment. By August 2013 that percentage had dropped to 63.2%. Economists have estimated that 3 to 5 million people have given up looking for work, not because they are old and want to retire, but because they have given up for the lack of good jobs.

CHAPTER 4

IMANI

Imani listened to her grandmother's breathing.
Each breath made a gurgling sound, and it seemed
like an eternity before the next breath would come.
With each exhale, Imani held her own breath, waiting for her grandmother's next inhale. This went on
for hours, the gurgling breaths and the eternal pauses
between them.

Seven of them sat around Grandma's bed in the tiny
room at the nursing home. They all sat in silence, listening to that terrible breathing, which the nurses called a
"death rattle." Imani's mother, Faith, and Aunt Benita
sat on the edges of the bed on either side of Grandma;
Imani's two sisters, Brenda and Lorraine, were sprawled
on the floor with their coloring books. Her cousins,

Jackson and Percy, Benita's teenage sons, stood leaning against the wall, looking down at their feet. The room was made all the more crowded by the machinery that monitored Grandma's heart rate; the sacks of liquid that connected to her veins through long, slender hoses; the large pouch of a thick, oatmeal-looking gruel that dripped through a larger tube into her stomach.

A nurse had called their house at ten that morning to tell them that Grandma was dying. She had fallen into a very deep sleep, and the nurse said to come to the nursing home right away because it might be the last time they could see her alive. It was a Sunday, when they should have been at church, but without Grandma there to scold them, they had decided to skip the service and sleep late. Aunt Benita was making her famous blueberry jelly waffles when the nurse called.

They dumped the waffles into the sink and hurried to the nursing home, where now they had been waiting for two hours. Imani's back ached from standing for so long. A nurse came in to check all the tubes connected to Grandma's body. That made the room even more crowded, so Imani asked her mom for a dollar and left to get a drink from the vending machine down the hall. She wanted a bottle of grape soda, but she knew Grandma would not approve—she never let the kids drinks sugary drinks. So instead, Imani pressed the button for a bottle of cold orange juice. That was the least she could do to show respect for her dying grandmother.

Imani heard a wail coming from her grandmother's room. Then more cries and sobs. She saw two nurses walking hurriedly toward the room. She started running back. Thoughts and fear raged inside her head. *No. Don't Die Grandma.* Grandma had always been there for her, for everybody. It was her house that gave them shelter. Her cooking that kept them fed. Her love that made them feel safe. Her strength that gave them courage. She couldn't die.

But she was dying and had been for some time. Nearly a year ago she started to lose weight. She would tire when playing hide-and-seek with Imani's two baby sisters. She had to ask Imani and her two cousins for help in the kitchen. She could no longer lift the big cast-iron skillets and pans that she used for her southern cooking, cooking that was famous in the Atlanta neighborhood where they lived. She was going to see the doctor a lot, and she kept insisting everything was all right. But it wasn't all right. She was getting so thin and throwing up all the time. Her hair was falling out. Finally, Imani's mom called the doctor and found out Grandma had cancer. It had started in her liver but had spread throughout her body. He was giving her drugs to try to kill the cancer, but those drugs made her ill and tired, and the cancer was still spreading.

"There is nothing more I can do," he said.

It got so bad that Grandma couldn't keep any food down. That was when the doctor said she had to go to the nursing home, where they would put a tube directly into her stomach to feed her and give her drugs to ease her pain. Grandma hated the humiliation of going to a nursing home. She hated all those tubes and machines. She hated being so weak that she couldn't even get out of bed to go to the bathroom by herself. Grandma got even worse after she went into the nursing home.

Now, three months later, she was gone.

Imani ran into the room and saw Aunt Benita draped over Grandma's now-still body, sobbing loudly. Jackson and Percy were standing on either side of her, rubbing her back. Momma stood in a corner, holding Brenda and Lorraine tight against her hips. Her body was shaking and tears were running down her cheeks, but she didn't make a sound. Imani went to her mother, wrapped her arms around her and the little girls, and held on tight.

They stayed like that for some time, frozen in their disbelief that Grandma was gone. Momma finally said that it was time to go.

"The nurses have to tend to Grandma now. There

is nothing more we can do for her," she said.

So each of them took a turn kissing Grandma on the forehead, gently, as her skin was as thin and white as fancy writing paper. Then Momma drove them all home in the family's old, beat-up minivan. Momma would be the head of the family now that Grandma was gone.

They drove slowly along the cracked, bumpy street of their old-Atlanta neighborhood. As they pulled into their driveway, they saw a man sitting on their front steps. Momma told everyone to go into the house, but Imani stayed with her mom. She didn't like the looks of that man.

As they approached him, Momma said, soft and sweet as a ripe Georgia peach, "May I help you?"

"Are you Faith Alma Jennings?" the man asked.

"No," Momma said, "I'm Faith Imani Jennings. Faith Alma Jennings is my mother."

"Well, I need to see her," the man said.

"You can't," Momma politely replied. "She passed away this afternoon."

The man's mouth dropped open, but nothing came out.

"What's this about?" Momma asked him, her voice less soft now.

"It's about the mortgage on the house," he said. "We

haven't received a payment for almost four months."

"What mortgage?" Momma asked, her voice hardening. "This house was paid for nearly twenty years ago."

"That's not right," the man said. "Your mother took out a $150,000 loan on this house about a year ago. I'm sorry she passed away, but we need to get paid."

"I don't know what you are talking about," Momma said. "She never said anything about a mortgage."

"Here's all the paperwork," the man said, giving Momma a thick yellow envelope. "We need to have payment in full in the next sixty days, or we are going to have to take this house away from you."

The man left. Imani sat down on the front steps with her mother. Momma's hands trembled as she opened the envelope. There were lots of papers inside. The one on top was a letter that said the family owed the mortgage company $10,000. This included four months of payments on the mortgage, which were $1,500 each for total of $6,000. It also included lots of "fees and penalties" because the payments were late, and also because the company said it needed to be paid back for having insurance protection on the house. These added up to another $4,000. The letter said in big bold letters that they had to receive the whole $10,000 in two months, or Imani and her family would lose their house.

"I don't understand," Momma said, her voice shaking. "Grandma must have taken out this loan when she found out she had cancer. I wondered where all the money came from that she had in her bank account. I thought she had saved it up. I had no idea she mortgaged the house."

"So can we pay them, Momma?" Imani asked.

"No," Momma said. "That money is all gone. We used it all up to pay for the drugs the doctor gave Grandma, plus all the bills from the nursing home. There's only about $2,000 left."

Momma worked as a nurses' aide at a hospital, and Aunt Benita worked part-time at a day care center. They worked hard, but they supported seven people with the money they made. There was never anything left over to save or pay for extras. The family spent it all just to keep food in their stomachs and clothes on their backs. Imani wanted her own cell phone in the worst way. Half of her friends at school had one, but Momma said they could just afford the bills for the one phone they had at home.

Imani could see Momma start to tear up. She grabbed her hand and squeezed it.

Momma turned to her and asked, "Where are we gonna get this kind of money?"

Imani didn't know what to say. Momma was always

the one with answers to her problems. Now she was asking Imani what to do.

But as soon as she asked the question, Momma's worried look changed. She smiled and said, "Don't worry, little bear. I will figure something out. I always do, don't I?"

"Yes you do, Momma," Imani said. And she felt better. Momma always did figure things out.

The rest of the week, Momma and Aunt Benita sat at the dining room table every night, with pieces of paper scattered in front of them. The pieces of paper were all the bills they paid every month. Water, electricity, gas, trash pickup. Receipts for groceries, Jackson's asthma medicine, Lorraine and Brenda's piano lessons, Percy's soccer team uniform and cleated shoes, Imani's Girl Scout dues and uniform. Imani never thought about all the money they spent each month on this and that. But there it all was, strewn across the dining room table. Momma and Aunt Benita decided that the family could do without cable TV, but they didn't want the kids to give up anything else. There were other expenses they could cut back on. Momma figured she could take the bus instead of driving to work, which would save on gasoline and parking. They could buy less expensive food, like beans and macaroni. But they still couldn't come up with enough to make the $1,500 monthly mortgage payment. So the only other answer was that they would have to make more money.

Momma decided to start working the night shift at the hospital. It paid more, and that way she could be home during the day to take care of all the kids. Aunt Benita said she could get full-time work at the day care center, which would bring in $850 more a month. Momma would make $500 more a month working the night shift, and by cutting back on expenses, that was just enough to make the $1,500 payment on the house loan, but they still didn't have the $10,000 that the man said the family already owed.

"Maybe they will let us pay that off bit by bit," Momma said one night to Aunt Benita. "It never hurts to ask."

So Momma called the phone number that was listed in all the paperwork the man had given her. She kept calling and getting recorded messages that told her to leave her name, phone number, and the code they had assigned to their mortgage: HXV728395. Every day she would call and leave the same message, but no one called her back. Then finally, after two weeks, a woman called her and said she was with the mortgage company, and that they were going to take away the house soon if she didn't pay the $10,000.

Momma tried to explain to her that she was late

on the mortgage because she didn't even know about it, and that Grandma had taken out the loan when she got sick, but all the money was spent on her medical bills. She explained that Aunt Benita was going to work extra so they could start making monthly mortgage payments, but they needed more time to pay the $10,000 that they already owed.

The woman said she couldn't help her. She only worked on foreclosures, but she gave Momma a phone number for a different part of the mortgage company, where she said they could help her get something called a "loan modification." "What's that?" Momma asked her, and the woman said, "It's a way to get your mortgage changed." So Momma called the number and got a new recording, but after several tries she finally connected with a real live woman who told her she should gather up all of her pieces of paper and send them to the mortgage company, and they would see what they could do.

Momma and Aunt Benita got together all of the pieces of paper the woman asked for. They gathered up three year's worth of bank account statements, tax returns, pay stubs, and their monthly bills. They also gathered up all of Grandma's medical bills. It was a pile of paper one inch thick, and it cost them $20 to have it copied before they sent it off to one of the mortgage company's offices in California. Momma didn't understand why she had to deal with someone in California, when the mortgage company had an office right there in Atlanta. But she did as the woman asked.

They waited and they waited to hear back from the woman. She never called. But the other woman, the one who said they were going to court to take back the house, kept calling. Momma started calling her the "foreclosure woman." The foreclosure woman said that Momma just had a few more weeks before they would have to "evict" her—a fancy way of saying they would kick the family out of the house. Momma and Aunt Benita were working so hard, but no one at that mortgage company seemed to care. They just kept threatening to take the house away.

Finally, the woman from the mortgage company who Momma called the "modification woman" phoned and said that they had received Momma's application to get help on the mortgage, but they had lost all the paperwork. Could Momma send it again? Momma had to go to work, so Aunt Benita stayed up all night putting all the papers together again, and Momma paid another $20 the next day to copy it and mail it to the mortgage company.

Then they waited. And waited. And waited. Nearly four weeks passed and they didn't hear from anyone.

Momma would try calling, but she would always get a machine telling her to leave a message. Imani was so scared that they were going to lose their house, but she tried not to let it show. With Aunt Benita working full-time, Imani kept herself busy working around the house more. She was a terrible cook, but she was good at laundry and she helped her little sisters with their homework in the evening. But that gave her less time for her own schoolwork. Imani had always been a straight-A student, but her grades started to slip. She was exhausted from helping around the house, and she couldn't sleep at night. As soon as she closed her eyes, her mind would race with worry about the family losing their home and having to live in their minivan, or one of those homeless shelters Imani had read about.

At last, Momma heard back from the mortgage company. But it was from the foreclosure woman, not the modification woman. She said a man was going to be out the next week to deliver a notice that the company was going to sell their house in an auction. Momma exploded on the phone. Imani had never heard her get so angry.

"We've begged you for help!" she shouted at the woman. "We've done everything you asked of us, and all you do is lose the papers we send you and refuse to call us back. For two months now we've managed to pay you $1,500 a month, even though we didn't even know about this mortgage. I told you that if you give us some time, I can pay that $10,000 you say we owe you too. But you are NOT putting us out of this house. If I have to chain myself and my children to the plumbing, you are NOT putting us out of this house."

Momma slammed the phone down, then went outside. She said she was going for a walk. She came back an hour later. Her face was red and her eyes were all puffy. It was time for her to go to work, so she showered and changed into her uniform, then kissed everyone good-bye, the way she always did.

"Don't worry," she said to Imani as she was leaving. "I'll figure something out. I always do."

Imani tossed and turned the whole night. The next day at school her math teacher called on her to answer a question, and Imani didn't even hear her, she was thinking so deeply about what would happen if they lost their house. When class was over, the teacher asked Imani to stay. Imani thought she was in trouble.

"What's going on, Imani?" she asked. "You look so exhausted. And you've been making mistakes on your tests and homework. You never used to do that. What's wrong?"

Then Imani blurted out the whole story about the mortgage company, and the people threatening to take away their house, and how her momma and aunt were working so hard and doing everything the mortgage company asked them to do, but they were still going to take away the house.

"I know someone who can help you," the teacher said. "There are lots of families like yours in Atlanta who are having the same problems. My church has formed a group of volunteers who can help you. They can stop this. You tell your momma I'm going to have somebody come over and see her tomorrow."

The next day a man named John Eakes came to their house. He sat and talked with Momma for two hours, and wrote down everything that she told him. He looked at all the papers and letters the mortgage company had sent them and looked at all the papers Momma had sent back, which the company kept losing. He took everything to make copies and said he would be back the next day.

Early the next morning Mr. Eakes came back with two other people, who were carrying a tent and sleeping bags! They pitched their tent on the front yard, and said they were going to stay there to protect Momma and her family until everything got sorted out. Then Mr. Eakes surprised Momma by telling her that a bunch of reporters from the local TV stations and newspapers were going to come by that afternoon to talk with her.

He told her, "Don't be nervous. Just tell them what you told me."

And so she did. Several vans came by at two that afternoon and unloaded cameras, lights, and big microphones. Momma stood on the house steps and told her story: how a man from the mortgage company came over the day Grandma died and threatened to take the house away; how she had called and called but had been ignored; how she and Aunt Benita were working to make the $1,500-a-month payments, which the mortgage company kept taking even though they still planned to take the house away; and about the $10,000 the company said she owed but wouldn't give her time to pay.

After Momma was done, Mr. Eakes announced that the church was going to court to stop the mortgage company from taking away the house, and that he and other church volunteers planned to sleep in their front yard so they could protect the house around the clock. He said the mortgage company was lying when it said Momma owed them $10,000, and he was going to ask the court to make the mortgage company pay Momma money because of all the pain and anguish they had caused her. He handed out a letter that a congressman had written to the head of the mortgage company, demanding to know why Momma, one of his constituents, had been so poorly treated.

Momma was in the newspaper and all the local news shows. The next day she got a call from the modification woman saying that they wanted to help her, but she had to stop talking to reporters. Then she told Momma that they couldn't find her paperwork, and that she needed to send it again. She also said that Momma now owed $12,000 because of the cost of insurance on the house. Momma asked her to hold on a minute and went out to the front yard to get Mr. Eakes. She gave him the phone, and he got on and told the woman that he would see her in court.

A few days later a man came to the house and gave Momma a letter from the mortgage company. He asked her to sign a piece of paper that said that she had received the letter. Mr. Eakes told her to go ahead and sign it. She opened the letter, and it said that the house was going to be auctioned off on the courthouse steps on the first Tuesday of the next month, which was just a month away.

Mr. Eakes told her not to worry. He said that he was going to get a hearing before a judge who could help stop the sale. He also said that he and two dozen other volunteers were going to the mortgage company's offices to stage a protest of the bad way the mortgage company had treated Momma. Imani asked Momma if she could go, but Mr. Eakes said they might get arrested, and he didn't want her in jail! He told Momma that Imani could watch from a safe distance across the street, and Momma agreed.

That afternoon Imani went down to the mortgage company's offices to watch the protest, along with her two cousins. It was three bus rides away, but she didn't care. She wanted to see what was going to happen. When she got there, she saw Mr. Eakes and his volunteers walking down the street carrying big signs that said STOP FORECLOSURES and PEOPLE FIRST. They were chanting, "Hey, hey, ho, ho, home foreclosures got to go." People standing on the sidewalks would whistle and clap their hands as the protestors walked by. When they reached the front door of the mortgage company's offices, they all sat down cross-legged in front of the building, about three rows deep, locking arms with one another. A mortgage company employee came out and asked them to leave, as no one could get into the building, but Mr. Eakes said they weren't budging until the president of the company came and told him personally that his company wouldn't foreclose on Momma's house.

Pretty soon the police came. Two big, strong police officers picked up each of the volunteers, one by one, and put them inside a large bus. Even though her momma had told her not to, Imani crossed the street and begged the police officers to let Mr. Eakes be. If he was in jail, he couldn't protect their house. Mr. Eakes smiled and told Imani to go on home, that he would be out in a few hours on bail.

True to his word, Mr. Eakes came back to the house that night and said he had good news. The judge had agreed to hear Momma's case. The only problem was that the date the judge set for Momma's hearing was after the date the mortgage company was going to auction. But Mr. Eakes said they had a way of stopping the auction, and Momma shouldn't worry.

The next day the protest at the mortgage company was all over the news. The modification woman called Momma again, complaining about Mr. Eakes and all the publicity. Then she said that the company would stop the foreclosure if Momma paid them $5,000 right away and the rest of the $12,000 in six months. Momma told her that wasn't enough time, and she was going to court because she didn't think she owed the company that much money.

Several weeks passed without any word from the mortgage company. Mr. Eakes's volunteers lived in their tents on the front yard the whole month as a sign of their commitment to protect Momma and her house. On the day the auction was going to take place, Mr. Eakes and his volunteers went down to the courthouse.

Mr. Eakes let Imani and her cousins go with them, on the condition, again, that they watch from the other side of the street. About a dozen people had gathered to bid on Momma's house, along with several other houses that were going to be auctioned that day. But when the auctioneer got to Momma's house, Mr. Eakes stood up and said that nobody should bid because the mortgage company had broken the law, and he and his volunteers were going to stay camped in the front yard until justice was done.

"Anyone who tries to buy this house," he told the crowd, "you are going to buy a dozen angry protestors living in your front yard. The Jennings family has lived in this house for over fifty years, and we are not going to let them lose it. The mortgage company took advantage of a sick, dying woman, lending her money they knew she couldn't pay back. Do you want to be part of this travesty of justice? Do you want to put the Jennings family out on the street?"

Everyone was looking down at their feet. No one wanted to look Mr. Eakes in the eye. When the auctioneer started asking for bids, nobody said a word.

"I guess you won't be selling this house today," Mr. Eakes said to the auctioneer.

They all went back to the house and gave Momma the good news.

"Our day in court is next week," Mr. Eakes said. "The judge is going to make things right."

The next week Momma, Imani, and the entire family—except for Aunt Benita, who had to work—put on their Sunday best and headed for the courthouse. Mr. Eakes said it would be good for the judge to see them. They arrived at the courthouse thirty minutes early and sat on wood benches outside the courtroom, patiently waiting for the court bailiff to call their name.

Finally, it was their turn. Mr. Eakes took Momma's hand and led her to a table facing the judge. There was a second table facing the judge, but no one sat there. The judge turned to Mr. Eakes and asked him where the mortgage company's attorneys were. Mr. Eakes said he didn't know. They had received notice that the hearing was set for today. Imani saw irritation in the judge's face.

"This is the seventh time in less than two months that the mortgage company hasn't shown up for a hearing," the judge said. "I am tired of them showing this court disrespect. State your case, Mr. Eakes, and I will decide based on the record before me."

So, Mr. Eakes told the judge all about the disrespect the mortgage company had shown Momma. How they wouldn't return her calls, how they would lose the papers she sent them, and how they were charging her thousands of dollars in fees and costs beyond what they were rightfully owed on the mortgage. He told the judge about how the mortgage company had made the loan to Grandma when she was sick and desperate, charging her an interest rate that was twice as high as mortgages they were giving other families. He pointed out that Momma had been making the mortgage payments on time ever since she found out about the loan, money that the mortgage company took even though they had planned all along to take away the house.

Imani could see the judge's face change from irritated to downright angry. "I think it's time to teach this company some respect, don't you?" he said with a wink to Momma.

Then the judge ordered the mortgage company to pay Momma exactly $12,000, which wiped out the debt Momma supposedly owed the company. And he ordered the company to lower Momma's mortgage payment so she was paying the same interest rate as most other families with mortgages. That brought the payment down to $1,200 a month.

Imani couldn't help herself. She let out a loud "ALL RIGHT!" Momma turned around and raised her fist high. Then everyone in the courthouse started applauding and whooping for Momma and congratulating the judge for what he had done. The judge had to bang his gavel on his desk at least ten times to quiet everyone down.

That night Mr. Eakes took the entire family out to dinner. The hospital had given Momma a day off because of her court appearance, so she was able to stay with them the whole evening. They went to Imani's favorite pizza parlor, and Imani snuggled up against her mother in one of the restaurant's red vinyl booths.

"I told you I'd think of something, little bear," Momma said to her, giving her a tweak on the nose.

"You always do, Momma," Imani said. She knew she had one brave mother.

WHY DID THE MORTGAGE COMPANY TREAT THE JENNINGS FAMILY SO BADLY?

As we discussed in earlier chapters, the process of securitization dramatically changed the way mortgages were made. Because mortgage originators did not have to suffer any of the loss if a borrower stopped paying on his or her mortgage, they became focused on making as many mortgages as possible, with little regard to whether the borrower could repay the loan. They were paid up front and had no responsibility if the borrower defaulted. So all they cared about was making as many mortgages as possible.

The separation of the decision to make a mortgage loan from the risk of losing money if the borrower stopped paying later on resulted in originators making millions of mortgages that borrowers were unable or unwilling to pay back. But it created another problem as well. When banks and thrifts made the loans and kept them, they were responsible for collecting the mortgage payments and working with borrowers who ran into trouble. This is called "loan servicing." And because the bank or thrift would suffer the losses if a troubled borrower stopped making payments, they had strong incentives to work with the borrower to keep up payments on the loan. A process called "loan modification" was widely accepted as a good business practice when a borrower ran into financial difficulty. Loan modifications usually meant the bank or thrift would reduce the borrower's payment, at least temporarily, until the borrower got back on his or her feet.

Helping troubled families with their mortgage payments was good for banks' reputations, but it also made good business sense. When homes are repossessed and sold in a foreclosure auction, they usually sell for much less than their true market value. After expenses the price can be 40% less than the true market price—that is, the price that similar houses are selling for in the same area. When homeowners voluntarily sell their homes, they will advertise it and let possible buyers come into their houses and look at the property. Interested buyers can hire professional home inspectors to make sure there is nothing wrong with the homes. However, bidders on foreclosed houses don't usually have a chance to inspect the houses, so they don't know exactly what they are buying. And sometimes when families are evicted, they get angry and damage the houses before they leave. So when people bid on foreclosed houses, the bids are low, because they don't always know what the house looks like on the inside and are worried that it might be damaged when the evicted family is forced to leave.

To illustrate why banks liked to do modifications, let's take the example of a house that is worth $200,000 based on the sales prices of similar houses in the same area. The family who owns the house is "underwater," meaning that they owe more than the house is worth; in this example, the amount they still owe the bank is $220,000. If the bank has to repossess the house and sell it at an auction, it expects to get a price that is only 60% of its market value. That is, it expects to be able to sell it for only $120,000, meaning that it will lose $100,000 on the loan.

60% of $220,000 = $120,000

$220,000 - $120,000 = $100,000 loss

In this case, it makes sense for the bank to lower the payments temporarily on the loan, hoping the family will work through their financial problems and catch up on the payments later on. In fact, the bank could reduce the amount on the loan to anything above $120,000, and still make more money than selling it at foreclosure.

But with securitization, thousands of investors owned the loans and the right to receive the payments on them, not individual banks. So the investors hired a "servicer" to collect payments on the loans and work with troubled borrowers on their behalf. The mortgage company dealing with Imani's family was one such service. These servicers were typically large financial institutions that had packaged and securitized the loans to begin with. Since the investors, not the servicers, suffered the losses if borrowers defaulted on their loans, the servicers had very little incentive to work with borrowers to try to keep them in their homes and do loan modifications that would avoid steep losses in a foreclosure sale.

What's more, servicers were not paid much to deal with troubled homeowners. They were paid a small amount for each loan they serviced, whether or not the borrower was troubled. Servicers could make money this way if all they had to do was collect payments every month and pass them on to investors. That didn't take much effort at all. But if borrowers fell behind on their mortgages, working with them was a much more expensive process. Servicers needed to hire more employees who could talk with borrowers on the phone, review their records to determine their financial condition, and figure out what kind of loan modification might work best for them. Servicers didn't want to spend money hiring a lot of staff to work with borrowers, because they weren't being paid enough to do so. And so what if the homes were sold in foreclosure sales at steep losses? The investors would suffer the losses, not the servicers.

The government tried to institute a number of programs to get servicers to modify more loans, but these programs only made a small dent in the problem. As millions of families started falling behind in their mortgage payments, servicers failed to hire enough employees to work with them. This is why it was so difficult for Imani's mother to reach someone at the mortgage company, and why they kept losing her paperwork. They simply didn't hire enough staff to answer all the phone calls and keep track of all the applications for modifications that they received.

The problem got so bad that servicers actually lost important documents showing that they had the right to foreclose. When they couldn't find those documents, they had junior employees swear in statements that they had the documents, when they really didn't. Junior employees would sign tens of thousands of these documents. The media called it "robo-signing," and several large servicers ended up paying billions of dollars to borrowers and the government because of this illegal practice. (More about that in Part 2.)

Even worse, some of these servicers tried to charge borrowers unjustified expenses. Once a home was sold in foreclosure, the servicer was paid back for certain expenses before investors received any of the money from the sale. One of these expenses was the cost of having property insurance on the house. Property insurance is very important to protect against losses to a house from damage by fire or theft, for instance. The cost of the insurance, called a "premium," is paid every month by the homeowner. Homeowners usually make a single payment every month that covers both the mortgage payment and the insurance premium (along with property taxes in some states). So when homeowners stop making their payments, not only do they fall behind on their mortgage, but they also lose their insurance coverage.

Once a family lost their insurance coverage, some servicers would then go buy much higher-priced insurance from an insurance company that they owned themselves. This is called "forced-placed" insurance. The servicer would charge very high rates—sometimes five times as much as the homeowner's old insurance policy—because it owned the company selling the insurance and therefore could make big profits. In Momma's case, the servicer was charging her $1,000 a month for this coverage. The government finally cracked down on servicers using their own insurance companies to charge homeowners huge premiums like these, but lots of people were hurt by the practice.

Fortunately for Momma, the mortgage company's understaffing and disorganization worked to her advantage in the end. The company was so disorganized, it didn't even show up in court to defend its position. This made the judge justifiably angry, so he gave Momma the relief she asked for, and Imani and her family got to keep their house.

HOW TO HELP HOMEOWNERS IN TROUBLE: MODIFICATION OR REFINANCING?

Jorge's and Imani's families were able to get loan modifications that reduced the monthly payments on their mortgages. It was relatively easy for Jorge's family to get a loan modification (once they asked) because a bank had made their loan and had not securitized it. If Jorge's dad stopped paying their mortgage, the bank would suffer the loss. So the bank was motivated to help Jorge's dad keep making some kind of payment on the mortgage to keep the family out of a costly foreclosure. The loan that had been made to Imani's grandma, however, was securitized. The mortgage company responsible for dealing with Imani's family did not have a stake in whether they paid the mortgage or went into foreclosure, so it really didn't care whether Imani's family got help. Throughout the financial crisis and its aftermath, banks that have kept the mortgage loans they made to families have done a much better job of helping troubled homeowners through modifications than those mortgage companies that have serviced securitized loans.

But what is a "modification"? A modification simply means that the terms of the mortgage loan are changed, or "modified." Modifications can take many forms. For instance, the lender can reduce the amount of money the borrower has to pay back. If a family owed $200,000 on their mortgage at an interest rate of 6%, the lender could say the borrower only has to repay $150,000. The amount a borrower owes on a loan is called "principal," and this kind of modification is called a principal reduction. Sometimes these principal reduction modifications are permanent, but sometimes the lender only agrees to defer the principal. This means that at the end of the loan term (usually 30 years), the borrower has to pay back the whole $50,000. This is known as a "balloon payment" because it is one, big bloated payment at the end.

Alternatively, the lender could reduce the interest rate on the loan from, say, 6% to 3%. This kind of modification is called an "interest rate reduction." Sometimes the interest rate reduction is permanent, but sometimes it is only temporary. For instance, the lender might agree to this reduced interest rate for a limited number of years—say, five years, for example. After five years the loan would revert back to its old rate of 6%.

Finally, the lender could just give the borrower more time to pay back the loan. For instance, it could extend the amount of time the borrower has to pay the loan from the typical 30 years to 40 years. This is called an "extended amortization" modification.

Each of these modifications can significantly reduce the monthly payment on a mortgage.

Let's start with an example of a $200,000, 30-year loan with a 6% interest rate. The monthly payment on that loan is $1,199.10.

By reducing the principal amount to $150,000,

the monthly payment is reduced to $899.33.

By reducing the interest rate to 3%, the monthly payment is reduced to $843.21.

By extending the repayment period to 40 years, the monthly payment is reduced to $1,100.43.

Responsible servicers will try to craft a loan modification for borrowers that gives them a payment that is realistic based on their income. This is also good business sense. If the modified payment is too high, the borrower will probably once again fall behind. This is called "re-default." Irresponsible servicers will try to squeeze as much as they can out of a troubled borrower. This is ultimately self-defeating as it simply leads the borrower to get into trouble again.

People frequently confuse a loan modification with a loan "refinancing." As we discussed in earlier chapters, a loan refinancing occurs when the borrower gets a completely new loan to pay off the old one. A refinancing can be done with a new mortgage originator or with the same one. In contrast, with a modification the borrower keeps the same loan, but some of its terms, like the interest rate or the amount that is owed—the principal—are changed.

In general a borrower cannot achieve a principal reduction through a refinancing, but can through a modification. When a loan is refinanced, the old loan has to be paid off in full. However, a refinancing can result in a lower interest rate.

HOW THE FEDERAL RESERVE HELPED SOME HOMEOWNERS LOWER THE INTEREST RATES THROUGH REFINANCINGS

In Chapter 1 we saw how families like Matt's were forced to refinance to avoid the much higher interest rates built into their mortgages. However, after the 2008 crisis a federal government agency called the Federal Reserve decided that it wanted to help borrowers refinance to get *lower rates* on their mortgages. The Federal Reserve is a system made up of twelve banks scattered across the country that other banks can go to when they need money. (Yes, just like you and your family have a bank, bankers have their own bank too, through the Federal Reserve System.) Sometimes a bank may fall short on cash. If the bank is healthy and can pay the loan back, the Federal Reserve lends it money.

But the Federal Reserve, or "Fed" as it is called, has an even more important job than being the "bankers' bank." It has the power to change interest rates and thus has the power to change how much it costs to borrow money. How does it do this? The answer is that the Fed can buy up securities, such as debt issued by our federal government, from people and institutions who currently own them. This lowers the interest rate that these securities must pay to find a willing buyer, which forces banks, in turn, to charge lower rates to people who borrow from them.

Where does the Fed get the money to make these purchases?

Guess what. It can create its own money!

In the past the Fed used its power to change interest rates primarily through lending it to healthy banks or through buying limited amounts of government securities from them or their customers (which would be deposited in banks). When the Fed buys securities or lends to a bank, it simply adds to the bank's account balance with the stroke of a computer key. In this way the Fed "creates money" and makes sure that banks always have plenty of cash to lend and meet other customer needs.

But after the 2008 financial crisis the Fed wanted to lower interest rates to help homeowners and other borrowers, so it did something pretty amazing. It started buying mortgage-backed securities. In fact, by the end of 2013 it had purchased $1.5 trillion worth of mortgage-backed securities, as well as $2.5 trillion of government securities. With all the money that the banks received through the Fed buying mortgage-backed and govern-ment securities, they had lots of cash to offer new mort-gages at very low interest rates.

The policy partially worked. The banks did make a lot of new mortgages to pay off old ones, allowing millions of people to refinance their mortgages at lower rates to reduce their monthly payments. Unfortunately, the banks didn't provide much new money at these low rates to help people buy houses. Instead, they just replaced old loans with new loans through refinancings. Banks left most of the additional money that the Fed's bond buying created in their own bank accounts at the Fed. Families trying to get loans to buy homes still had trouble getting mortgages.

Though millions of people were helped by the Fed's actions, most of the people who had fallen behind on their payments were not able to take advantage of them. Because of all the losses on mortgages that occurred dur-ing the financial crisis, banks were scared to make new loans for people to buy houses or to refinance borrowers who were having trouble with their current mortgages. The latter group had to look to loan servicers for help with modifications. And because the servicers were so under-staffed, millions of people who needed help couldn't get it.

Though many people were unable to refinance to take advantage of the lower rates, the ones who could refinance received substantial benefits. In 2008 the average rate on a 30-year, fixed-rate loan available to people with good credit was 6%. By 2013 that rate had dropped to 4%. So on a $100,000 mortgage, reducing the interest rate from 6% to 4% would reduce the monthly payment from $755 to $634. (Of course, the banks providing these refinancings also made a lot of money from the refinancing fees.)

Because the economy was hurt so badly by the financial crisis, the Fed decided to buy unprecedented amounts of government bonds and mortgage-backed securities. Before the crisis the Fed held about $900 billion worth of securities. At the end of 2013 the Fed held over $4 trillion worth of securities and was still buying, though it was reducing the amount it purchased each month.

By making it cheap to borrow, the Fed hoped that it could encourage consumers to spend more and businesses to invest and grow. Unfortunately, while there have been some benefits from the lower interest rates, our overall economy has not improved very much. And while the Fed has very good intentions, some fear that by making it so cheap to borrow, the Fed will encourage households and businesses to once again take on too much debt. Others say, however, that if the Fed had not made it so cheap to borrow, our economy would be in even worse shape.

CHAPTER 5

MARY

"Next year's sixth-grade class is 20% larger than this year's class of graduating eighth graders. If 260 eighth graders are graduating, how big is the incoming sixth-grade class?"

Mary's palms were wet and clammy. Her stomach was tight as a knot. She hated word problems. Her brain froze every time she read one. How could she figure out how big a sixth-grade class was based on how big an eighth-grade class was? How big was the seventh-grade class, she wondered? Did that matter? She was in the seventh grade. But she sure couldn't figure out this problem.

Her teacher, Mr. Miller, used to walk up and down the aisles when he gave an open-book test and answer kids' questions when they raised their hands. He wouldn't give away the answers, but he would always give them a little hint or two that would help them figure it out on their own. But he didn't have time to do that now. Mary's class size had grown from twenty kids to thirty-five kids. Mr. Miller had tried to keep helping Mary and her classmates, but he couldn't help everyone who had questions during the fifty minutes that was allotted for pre-algebra. It wasn't fair to help only some kids, so he just stopped helping everybody.

Mary tried to remember how to do percentages. How much was 20% of 260? Did she multiply 20 times 260? That didn't make any sense. That would be 5,200 students. Nobody's class was that big. She seemed to recall something about decimal points. Yes, that was it. She multiplied 260 by .20. That gave her 52 students, not 5,200. She wrote 52 down as her answer, hoping against hope it was right.

Mary was very good at English and history. She got As in those courses. But she always struggled with math, and each year the classwork seemed to get harder and harder. She had done much better when there were fewer students in her class. Mr. Miller had more time to answer each student's questions, and she loved the way he would do it quietly while walking the aisles. Questions and answers could be spoken in soft whispers that no one else needed to hear. Mary was so afraid that other students would think she was dumb if they heard her questions (even though Mr. Miller insisted there were no dumb questions). The school used to have a math tutor who students could go see after school for help with their math homework. Mary went to see the tutor a lot, but the school had to let her go. The principal said they just didn't have enough money to pay her.

Getting rid of the math tutor wasn't the only way Mary's school was cutting back on expenses. They had turned down the heat to 65 degrees to save money on heating bills. But Chicago winters were cold, and it was hard for Mary to stay warm just sitting at a desk in a classroom, despite several layers of underwear, sweaters, and socks. They cut after-school sports, too, so Mary could no longer play soccer in the school league. She and her friends still got together to kick the ball around, but it just wasn't the same as an organized team with a coach. Some of the cuts seemed just plain silly, like no toilet paper or paper towels in the bathroom. Now everyone carried little tissue packets to school with them.

Year after year, beginning in 2009, Mary's school kept cutting and cutting. But at least the school stayed open. The school district had closed Mary's little sister's grade school and combined it with another school that was a lot farther from their house. Mary's sister had to get up thirty minutes earlier in the morning to make it to school on time.

When Mr. Miller returned the graded test to Mary, she saw that she had a C-. She had missed half of the problems, including the one that asked about the growing sixth-grade class.

"You needed to add the 52 to 260 to get the right answer," Mr. Miller had scribbled in the margin. "The correct answer was 312. See me after school."

Mary dropped by Mr. Miller's classroom after school was over that day. He smiled as he saw her enter the room.

"Your grades have been going down," he told her. "Some of the other students have been struggling too, since the school ended the math tutoring program. I've decided to start having a math session at my house on Saturday mornings. Here is the address. Come over at nine this Saturday morning."

Mary dropped her books on the desk with a loud thump and gave a surprised Mr. Miller a big hug around the neck. "Thank you," she said excitedly. "Thank you soooo much."

Every Saturday morning after that, Mary and five of her classmates went to Mr. Miller's house, where he answered their questions and helped them work through problems from the week before. She felt bad that Mr. Miller had to sacrifice his Saturday mornings for her and her classmates. She knew they were taking weekend time that he would otherwise spend with his family. But she was so grateful he was willing to help. She even managed a B- in pre-algebra by the end of the school year.

WHY WAS MARY'S SCHOOL CUTTING BACK ON EXPENSES?

Why would schools be affected by lots of bad mortgage lending decisions? The schools didn't have anything to do with the financial crisis. They didn't take out unaffordable loans. Why would they be cutting back?

The impact of the financial crisis turned up in many unexpected places. One was in school cutbacks. To explain this, you need to first understand where schools get their money to operate.

In most parts of the country, schools derive a big part of their budgets from property taxes. A property tax is usually collected by a county, and it is typically calculated by applying a small percentage to the value of someone's house. Property taxes vary widely around the country, ranging from less than .2% to 2.0%. For instance, if the value of a person's house was $100,000, and the property tax rate was .2%, the amount of the tax would be $200 a year. If the tax rate was 2.0%, the amount of the tax would be $2,000 a year. (Hopefully you will understand these calculations and, unlike Mary, will not be confused by where to put your decimal points!)

What happens when the values of houses go down? Since property taxes are based on the value of a house, if the value of the house goes down, so does the amount of money collected to support public schools. Nationally, home prices declined by over 30% from their peak in 2006 to their lowest point in 2012. So, for instance, if the value of the house in our example above decreased from $100,000 to $70,000 (a 30% reduction), property taxes collected would also decrease by 30%. If the tax rate was .2%, the new amount collected would be $140. It would be $1,400 if the rate was 2.0%. In both cases these are big reductions.

Public schools were hit hard by declining property tax values. But schools also receive money from state income taxes. Most states have an income tax (as does the federal government). This is simply a requirement that people pay a percentage of their income to the state to support government services. States usually take some part of the money they collect from income taxes and give it to schools to support their operations.

But as we saw with Jorge's dad in Chapter 3, lots of people lost their jobs during the Great Recession. And when they lost their jobs, they lost income, which reduced the amount of money that states could collect from them in income taxes. State income taxes generally range from 4% to as high as 10%. For instance, Jorge's dad's monthly income was reduced from $6,000 to $2,000. If his state applied a 10% tax rate, the amount of revenue collected would have dropped from $600 to $200 a month. (Actually, the amount may have dropped even more because most states will reduce the rate they apply, the lower the family's income, as they should.)

The Great Recession had a terrible impact on money that the government could collect in taxes to support public schools. To be sure, school districts had (and continue to have) other problems. But reduced taxes because of home price declines and increased unemployment took their toll. The total amount of money the government collected to support schools and other functions dropped by nearly 20% in 2008 and 2009. Most states had to cut back on the amount of money they spent on students. In many states those cuts exceeded 10%.

Elementary and secondary schools were not the only places where states were forced to cut back on services. Budget cuts were felt across the board. States cut spending by 3.8% in 2009 and 5.7% in 2010, compared to a general trend of 1.6% growth in the years prior to the crisis. Public assistance programs for the poor and elderly, public transportation systems, and subsidies for state colleges and universities also suffered significant cutbacks. In addition, funds many states used to give temporary support to unemployed workers ran out of money, forcing states to borrow $50 billion from the federal government. So not only were families confronting the prospect of lost jobs and lost homes as a result of the crisis, they were also suffering from a reduction in public services and safety net programs provided by their local governments. These cutbacks in services worsened the emotional toll, stress, and anxiety of kids and their parents who were already struggling to get by.

CHAPTER 6

ZACH

"When will you be home, Ian?"

Zach saw his brother's back stiffen when his mother asked the question, a question she always asked him every time he went out at night.

"Not sure, Mom," Ian answered. "Don't wait up. It could be late."

"Are you going out with Christy?" their mother asked. "When are we going to get to meet her?"

Why doesn't she leave him alone? Zach thought to himself. *He's twenty-three years old.*

"Soon, Mom," Ian answered, forcing a smile. "It's just that she lives really far away, and it's inconvenient to drive all the way over here. Maybe we can all meet at a restaurant sometime."

Zach knew why Ian didn't want to bring Christy over. She didn't know that Ian still lived at home. Ian tried to keep that a secret from everyone. He was humiliated that he was still living with his parents.

When Ian graduated from high school, his parents couldn't afford to send him to college. So he was going to have to borrow money to go to school. At first he thought he might get a job and work for a few years to save money to go to school. But he couldn't find a job with only a high school education. Everybody he talked to told him he needed a college degree. His parents wanted him to enroll at the state public university that was located in their hometown of Ft. Collins, Colorado.

"The tuition is only about $5,000 a year," Zach remembered his dad saying. "And you can live at home to save on expenses."

But the last thing Ian wanted to do was live at home with his parents. He loved his parents, but Dad was always trying to tell him what to do, and Mom was really nosy. Plus, some school in Denver had been calling him a lot, trying to get him to enroll there. It was a lot more expensive than the state university, but they offered a degree in building design, and Ian had always dreamed of being an architect. The school said it would take only a few years to graduate, and then he could get work designing buildings, making over $200,000 a year. He wouldn't be a full-fledged architect, but they said this degree was just as good, and it wouldn't take as long to get. They sent him videos of other students who said they had graduated from their school, bragging about how easy it was to find a job and how much money they made.

Best of all, the school's recruiters told him, Ian could borrow all the money that he needed to go to their school, because the federal government would guarantee all the loans. The recruiters said that he could also borrow the money he needed to live on their campus, as Denver was a long drive from his house. So without telling his parents, Ian enrolled at the school.

Dad blew up when he found out. "That place is going to charge you over $70,000 for your degree, and that doesn't even include your living expenses." Ian showed him all the brochures the school had given him, and the videos of other students who had graduated. Dad just shook his head. "These people are taking advantage of you." But Ian was convinced that he had done the right thing.

Unfortunately, Dad turned out to be right. With the tuition, combined with the fees he paid for books and to live on campus, Ian piled up nearly $100,000 in debt. And when he graduated, he couldn't find a job anywhere. All of the Denver architectural firms he talked to said that he had to have a real architectural degree to work for them. The best job he could find was at a hardware store back in Ft. Collins.

Ian had to pay $700 a month on his loans, and he only brought home $1,200 a month working at the hardware store. Since $500 a month was not enough to live on, he ended up moving back home. Knowing that their father had been right about the school in Denver made the situation even more humiliating for Ian.

Zach was relieved that their dad never said "I told you so." And Zach felt guilty about it, but he loved the fact that Ian was back home sharing a room with him again. They would stay up late at night talking. Ian would give him hints about how to talk to a girl Zach liked in his seventh-grade class. Zach would crack up when Ian told stories about Mr. Sutter, the chubby manager at the hardware store where he worked, who was trying to lose weight by eating nothing but green vegetables. All those vegetables made Mr. Sutter very flatulent. "We've lost 20% of our customers since he started his diet," Ian would joke.

But Zach knew how miserable Ian was living at home and badly wanted to help him.

One Saturday, Zach was over at their neighbor Mrs. Neiman's house to mow her lawn, as he was every other weekend. As usual, he had to struggle to pull the mower, rake, and wheelbarrow out of her overcrowded garage, and when he was finished, it was another big struggle to put it all back. As he approached her front door to collect the $20 she paid him, he was struck with an idea. As she handed him the money, he took a deep breath. "You know, Mrs. Neiman, it is really hard to get the mower in and out of your garage. If I didn't have to do that, I would charge you $5 less. Why don't you build a shed in your backyard for all of your yard equipment?" he asked her. "My brother, Ian, could design it and build it for you. He's really good at building things."

Mrs. Neiman looked at him thoughtfully.

"That's an excellent idea, Zach," she said. "You tell your brother to come see me."

That night Zach gave Ian the good news over dinner. "It's just a small job," he said, "but it could lead to more work around the neighborhood."

He could tell that Ian was pleased. Ian went to see Mrs. Neiman the very next day. He ended up building her the best shed anyone ever had, with a ramp and big, wide barn doors that made it so easy to get the mower in and out—she could do it herself, and she was seventy years old. He also installed windows on one side of the shed with pretty flower boxes under them, where Mrs. Neiman planted red and white begonias.

Word spread, and soon Ian picked up more work

around the neighborhood. A patio for Mr. Sellers, a carport for the Whitney family, a deck for the Allisons. Ian would make meticulous designs for each project—as if he were building the Taj Mahal—and then would take photographs of it once it was finished.

After Ian completed several jobs around the neighborhood, he gathered up all the designs and photos of them and showed them to architecture firms in Denver. It took him several weeks of visiting these firms, but he finally found one that was willing to hire him as an apprentice, which Zach understood to be a kind of architect-in-training. After several months they were so impressed with Ian's work that they agreed to pay his tuition to take architecture classes at night at the state university. Ian was disappointed to discover that none of the classes that he took at the school in Denver were recognized by the state university, so he would have to start from scratch in building credits for an architecture degree. With the architecture firm helping him, he would eventually get an architecture degree, though it would take many years.

Ian was finally making enough money at the firm to get a small apartment in the suburbs between Denver and Ft. Collins. Once he was no longer living at home, he brought Christy over to the house (and their mom adored her).

Ian was doing well, with a girlfriend, a job, and a path to becoming a real architect. He was happy, and Zach felt proud that he had helped.

WHY COULDN'T IAN FIND WORK?

The 2008 financial crisis caused millions of people to lose their jobs. About 5% of American workers were unemployed prior to the crisis, but that rate jumped up to 10% by the end of 2009. By the fall of 2014 it had dropped to 5.9%, though this is still high by historical standards for an economy in recovery. Unfortunately, a lot of the improvement in the unemployment rate since the crisis has come from people getting frustrated and dropping out of the workforce. And even when people can find work, the jobs usually pay less than those they had prior to the crisis.

Youth unemployment has been an even bigger problem. Defined by the government as the percentage of people ages 16 to 24 who are looking for work but can't find it, the youth unemployment rate soared from about 10% prior to the crisis to over 18% in 2010. By the fall of 2014 it remained at a stubbornly high 14.3%. For black youth, the rate was 24.8%, and for Hispanic youth, it was 16.8%.

Why is unemployment so high among young

people? Why have they been having a tougher time finding a job than older workers have been?

As businesses cut back on jobs during the Great Recession, the job market became more competitive. That is, there were a lot more people looking for jobs because they had been laid off, and fewer jobs that were available. That meant that employers could be a lot pickier. So they tended to favor hiring people who had job experience and a proven track record in the workforce. Young people like Ian, who were just graduating, had no job experience or track record, so they were assumed to be less desirable by employers. Another problem: Older workers, who might have otherwise decided to retire, stayed in the workforce longer because they lost money and wealth during the Great Recession. For instance, the value of retirement savings for workers nearing retirement plummeted by 30% as a result of the Great Recession. Older people were also hit by falling home prices, as a lot of retirees were planning on partly paying for their retirement by selling their houses. But with home prices down, they couldn't sell them for as much as they were planning to.

Ian was smart to go to college, because the unemployment rate among college graduates is half the rate among young people who only have a high school diploma. However, as Ian discovered, some degrees are worth a lot, and some aren't worth much at all. In the wake of the Great Recession the federal government significantly expanded the amount of financial aid available for young people to go to school. It started lending money directly to students to go to college, to make student loans more widely available and cheaper than they had been when private lenders did the lending. Congress also greatly expanded higher education benefits available to young people who had served in the military, with cash assistance provided to young veterans to pay for books and tuition as well as cover their living expenses.

Unfortunately, a number of for-profit companies decided to take advantage of young people who could now easily borrow money to go to college. (Public colleges and universities are operated by state and local governments as nonprofits, meaning that they are partially funded by taxpayers and do not charge tuition and fees beyond what they need to cover faculty salaries and other expenses. A for-profit college, on the other hand, is privately owned and tries to make money for the school's owners.) There are many good colleges that operate as for-profits. There are many others that are really more interested in making money through government student aid programs than they are about providing a good education to young people.

Congress has long been worried about for-profit schools trying to take advantage of student aid programs, so many years ago it required that at least 10% of for-profit colleges' students had to pay for school without federal government assistance. In this way, Congress hoped to limit federal student aid to only those schools with degree programs that were good enough to attract students paying on their own. However, because of a technical problem with the way the law was written, members of the military who were receiving assistance to go to school could count in that 10%. So, these unscrupulous schools started vigorously recruiting veterans who qualified for military aid. There have been many reports of abuses, including one for-profit school that enrolled brain-damaged veterans who could not even remember the courses they were enrolled in.

A study conducted by a committee of the US Senate found that for-profit colleges are much more expensive than state schools, even though they have lower graduation rates and their graduates have a harder time finding good jobs than graduates of state schools. For instance, this report found that one year the government spent $697 million to send veterans to state schools and $640 million to send veterans to for-profit colleges. However, that $697 million to state schools paid for more than 200,000 veterans to go to school, while the $640 million to for-profit colleges only educated about 76,000 veterans.

In a lawsuit filed by the State of California, one big for-profit school was charged with giving young people false information about how many of its students got jobs once they graduated. This lawsuit said that the for-profit school actually paid a temporary employment agency to hire its graduates for a short period of time so that the school could boost the number of graduates who supposedly got jobs!

It is very sad that there are dishonest companies who would take advantage of young people trying to better themselves with a good education. Ever since the financial crisis, young people—confronted with a difficult job market—have been taking on more and more debt to go to college to try to improve their employment prospects. They shouldn't have to worry about also being exploited by greedy schools. Total student debt stood at about $550 billion in early 2007. But by mid-2014 it had ballooned to $1.2 trillion. Two-thirds of students now graduate from college with debt. The average amount that they owe is around $29,000, which is about 60% of the average annual pay of young college graduates. So while it is good that more and more young people can get loans to go to college, they need to be careful about the school they go to and the degree they obtain, because repaying those loans will take a big chunk of their income. Ian made a mistake. He racked up $100,000 of debt for a degree that was worthless, and it will be many, many years before he has paid off that debt. Unfortunately, his situation is not that unusual.

The huge increase in student debt is not only a burden for graduating students. It could also hurt the economy. If graduates have to spend a lot of their income repaying their student loans, they will have less money to spend on other things—like buying a car or taking out a mortgage to buy a home. It could also become a problem for taxpayers, who will suffer the losses if those graduates can't afford to pay back their loans. About 44% of student borrowers have already delayed repaying their loans because they have received approval from the government based on their financial situations. Of graduates who are supposed to be repaying their loans, at the end of 2013, 13.7% had defaulted on their payments.

PART 2
MY STORY

CHAPTER 7

THE CAST OF PLAYERS

On October 13, 2008, a very important meeting was held in a big conference room at the US Treasury Department. The Treasury Department is that part of our government responsible for the nation's finances. It has many responsibilities, but its main job is to make sure the government has enough money to operate. It does this by collecting taxes or by borrowing money when tax money isn't enough to support government spending. It is also responsible for helping to make sure that our financial system functions properly.

A man named Henry Paulson was the secretary of the Treasury Department on October 13, 2008. Prior to his time at the Treasury, Paulson had run Goldman

Sachs, one of the largest and most prestigious investment banks in the world. Though he had spent most
of his career on New York's Wall Street, he actually
grew up on farms in rural Illinois. He played football
and was active in Boy Scouts, attaining an "Eagle" rank.
Paulson—or "Hank" as he was known to his friends
and colleagues—had spent most of his career in investment banking, which helped him to understand the
problems that were now plaguing our financial system.
Some people thought that because of his background,
he viewed those problems too much from the perspective of Wall Street banks. That may be true, but based
on my experience working with him, I think he also
remembered his Main Street roots.

Paulson was very worried that the US economy was
getting into deep trouble because our financial system
was not functioning properly. A big investment bank—
Lehman Brothers—had just gone into bankruptcy, and
this was causing serious problems. Lehman Brothers
had securitized many bad loans and had invested in a
lot of risky mortgage securities and derivatives. When
it went into bankruptcy, the investors and other financial institutions that had lent Lehman Brothers money
realized they were going to take big losses. When other
investors saw this happening, they became reluctant to
lend to any big financial institution that owned a lot of

mortgage securities and derivatives. Unfortunately, that was most of them! In fact, it was getting so bad that big financial institutions weren't even sure that they wanted to lend to one another.

Paulson was worried that if any more of these big financial institutions went into bankruptcy, investors would get so scared that no one would lend to any of them, and they would all get into trouble, even the healthy ones that didn't do stupid things. Something similar happened in the 1930s, when depositors lost confidence in all the nation's banks and pulled their money out of those banks in what is called a "bank run." But depositors weren't the problem now. Because of the agency that I headed, the Federal Deposit Insurance Corporation, most bank depositors were protected by the government, so they were leaving their money in the banks. Yet deposits weren't the only place where big financial institutions got money to operate. They also borrowed from one another and from investors by issuing debt, a kind of IOU. And the big institutions that lent money to banks and investors who bought their debt were now getting scared.

So Paulson called the heads of the nine biggest banks in the country to the Treasury for a meeting to discuss how we could get our financial system working again. He also asked the heads of the government agencies that had a role in regulating these banks to come to the meeting. That included me in my capacity as chairman of the Federal Deposit Insurance Corporation, or FDIC. Though my agency did not have direct responsibility for regulating these big banks, we did provide government insurance for trillions of dollars of money that businesses and households had on deposit with them, so obviously we had some interest in their financial health.

I got to the meeting early, and I was very nervous. To help keep the financial system functioning, Paulson had asked my agency to temporarily guarantee the debt of these big banks so that investors would keep lending them money. I was going to announce the program at the meeting. Most people think of banks for their role in lending money to households and businesses, but banks are big borrowers, too. Many of these nine banks had to borrow money on a daily basis to keep operating. Most of them seemed reasonably healthy and would be able to make good on all their debts. But others, I thought, were not in good shape and might not be able to repay all the debt that they issued. In that case, the FDIC would have to pay. This was a big risk for us.

The sickest bank was a big institution called Citigroup, or "Citi." It was run by a man named Vikram Pandit, whom I did not think was qualified because he had no past experience as a banker. Citi had done just about every dumb thing there was to do in the years leading up to the crisis. The board of Citi had removed the previous head of the bank but inexplicably replaced him with Pandit, an unsuccessful hedge fund manager with no real banking experience. I suspected that the Citi board hired him because one of its most powerful members, a man named Bob Rubin, wanted him to have the job. Rubin was a former secretary of the Treasury himself and, like Paulson, had once headed Goldman Sachs. Rubin had done many positive things when he was secretary of the Treasury under President Bill Clinton. But once he left to become a leading member of Citi's board, he had encouraged Citi to take many of the risks that had gotten it into trouble. Regrettably, he still had a lot of influence at the bank.

Pandit glared at me as I entered the room. He had tried but failed to get the FDIC to help him buy another, smaller bank that we insured called Wachovia. Wachovia was losing money on a lot of bad mortgages and business loans. But I was worried that letting Citi buy Wachovia would be a little like asking one drunk to lean up against another to keep him upright! Citi had deep problems of its own. A very healthy bank called Wells Fargo was also interested in buying Wachovia and wanted no FDIC assistance to do so. So it was better for the FDIC if Wells bought Wachovia instead of Citi buying the bank.

The head of Wells Fargo, Dick Kovacevich, rushed over to talk with me as soon as I entered the room. He wanted to give me an update on Wells's purchase of Wachovia. He was very proud of the fact that Wells had just sold a lot of new stock to help it pay for the bank, which was a good sign. It showed that stock investors had confidence in Wells's strength and management. I respected Kovacevich. He had grown up in a small lumber town in Washington State, and had worked his way up to head one of America's biggest banks. He was an experienced banker who was doing a good job managing Wells. But sometimes he and I disagreed over regulation. When it came to regulators, Dick was kind of like that kid in class who always raises his hand to give the teacher trouble. Dick was smart and he just didn't want anyone having power over him or telling him what to do, and that included regulators.

Half listening to Dick, I looked across the room to see three other bankers in a group talking with one another. Towering over the group was Jamie Dimon, who ran JPMorgan Chase. Dimon was a native New Yorker and grandson of Greek immigrants. His father and grandfather were both stockbrokers. He was an imposing man in both height and stature. Known as tough and smart, he had anticipated problems in the mortgage market in early 2006 and took steps to protect his bank. As a result, when the mortgage market started to go bad, Dimon's bank remained healthy. In fact, like Wells, he was able to scoop up other troubled banks for bargain prices. One of those was Bear Stearns, which Dimon bought with help from the New York Federal Reserve Bank. Another was Washington Mutual, or "WaMu," a troubled mortgage lender that the FDIC seized to protect WaMu's depositors. We auctioned the bank off to healthier banks, and JPM Chase was by far the highest bidder, paying us nearly $2 billion for that sick thrift institution. Chase also committed to protect all of WaMu's depositors. If the FDIC had not been able to find a buyer for WaMu, it would have cost us $40 billion.

Dimon was widely respected for the way he had made good buys for Chase while also helping the government. A few years later, however, he would stumble badly, when his bank suffered big losses on derivatives trades. But on that day he was viewed as Wall Street's king of the roost.

Joining him in conversation was Lloyd Blankfein, the current head of Goldman Sachs, who stood about a foot shorter than Dimon but was every bit as tough and pugnacious. Unlike Dimon, who came from wealth and attended private schools, Blankfein's dad worked for the Postal Service, and Blankfein went to public schools. He had the funniest wit on Wall Street, with twinkling eyes and an elfish grin. Have you ever read *A Midsummer's Night's Dream* by William Shakespeare? I always thought that Puck would look just like Lloyd Blankfein.

Goldman Sachs was in reasonably good shape, though it was suffering losses on its mortgage investments. But Blankfein had been able to convince legendary investor Warren Buffett to invest in his bank to help tide it over. With Warren Buffett's seal of approval and money behind it, Goldman was likely to survive.

Also in the group was John Mack, who headed the second biggest investment bank after Goldman, a firm called Morgan Stanley. Mack was the son of Lebanese immigrants. His father ran a grocery store in Mooresville, North Carolina. Mack went to Duke University and eventually landed in New York, joining Morgan Stanley in 1972. Though he lived in New York most of his life, he never lost his southern drawl. Most of these Wall Street bankers talked in the rapid-fire style of the typical New Yorker, but Mack drew out his words slowly. His southern charm, like Blankfein's wit, could be disarming, but both could be ruthless when they needed to be.

Like Blankfein, Mack had been able to find a rich investor to help his bank. It was a big Japanese bank called Mitsubishi. With the deep pockets of that Japanese giant behind it, Morgan Stanley was also likely to survive.

Not so for another investment bank called Merrill Lynch. Merrill had invested heavily in risky mortgage derivatives and securities. Even into 2007, when problems in the mortgage market were becoming more and more obvious, Merrill Lynch kept making bigger and bigger bets on the housing market, and it used lots of borrowed money to do so. Deeply in debt and losing money fast, Merrill had fired its former head and replaced him with a relatively young investment banker (also a former Goldman executive) by the name of John Thain. Thain's job was hopeless, and the first thing he did was to arrange a sale of Merrill to Bank of America. Thain now stood on the perimeter of the Dimon-Blankfein-Mack group, trying to listen in on their conversation. I was surprised that he had been invited to the meeting, as he had been the head of Merrill for such a short period, and would no longer be the top executive once Merrill was sold to Bank of America.

Bank of America's head, Ken Lewis, stood awkwardly alone at one end of the big ornate conference table that dominated the room, busying himself by leafing through some papers. He didn't really seem to fit in with the New York bankers. They viewed him, somewhat, as a country bumpkin. He was good at running a commercial bank but not so good at making deals. In addition to buying Merrill Lynch, he had also bought a mortgage lender called Countrywide Financial. Countrywide was the leading originator of subprime and other risky mortgages, while Merrill Lynch was a leading packager of those mortgages into securities. Both institutions were in bad trouble, and in my opinion, Lewis had not done his homework and was paying way too much for both. His bank was healthy at that point, but would soon be dragged down by these overpriced purchases. Indeed, five years after the crisis, Bank of America would continue to struggle with the consequences of Countrywide's bad lending.

At the other end of the conference table stood Robert Kelly, the head of Bank of New York, or "BoNY," and Ronald Logue, the head of State Street Corporation. I had never met Logue. Kelly I knew primarily by reputation. He was known as a conservative banker with Canadian roots. Highly competent but a bit full of himself. The banks that he and Logue headed were not nearly as big as the others, but they were still very important because as "trust" banks they managed trillions of dollars of their customers' money.

The room became quiet as Hank Paulson entered, followed by Ben Bernanke, the chairman of the Federal Reserve Board, and Tim Geithner, the president of the New York Federal Reserve Bank. I liked and respected Ben Bernanke. He was a thoughtful person, a good public servant who cared deeply about the country. Maybe that came from his modest upbringing. He grew up in Augusta, Georgia. His father was a pharmacist, and his mother was an elementary school teacher. A brilliant student (he scored 1590 out of 1600 on his SATs), he attended college at Harvard and got his PhD in economics from MIT. From there he became a tenured professor at Princeton and the country's foremost authority on the Great Depression. Having studied the financial crisis that brought on the Great Depression in 1929, Ben could understand the perils that the country now faced in 2008.

As much as I admired Ben (though we didn't always agree), I couldn't say the same of his subordinate, Tim Geithner. The Federal Reserve system is made up of a seven-member board that is based in Washington and headed by the chairman. Under the board is a network of twelve regional banks that are responsible for carrying out the Fed's regulatory responsibilities. They also carry out the Fed's job as a "banker's bank"—making sure that banks have enough cash to function. Since most of the biggest banks are located in New York and thus regulated by the New York Reserve Bank, it is by far the most influential and powerful among the twelve banks in the Fed system.

Tim and I had clashed a lot. I felt that he was too concerned about the profitability of the big banks he regulated and not enough about holding them accountable when they did stupid things. (More about that later.) He and I had also clashed over how to deal with Citi. He had once worked for Bob Rubin at the Treasury Department and remained close to him. I knew that he had been talking with Rubin about Citi's problems and was determined to find a way for the government to help that troubled institution. He became very angry with me when I refused to help Citi buy Wachovia and stop the Wells acquisition. He was hoping that with FDIC support, investors would regain confidence in Citi and be more willing to lend it money and invest in its stock. He did not seem worried about the risks to the FDIC, and he did not seem to understand that our primary mission was to protect depositors, not big Wall Street banks. Hank and Ben always tried to see things from my point of view, and did not fault my decision to let the Wells purchase proceed. But Tim still held a grudge.

Everyone took their seats, and Hank got right to

the point. The public was losing confidence in the financial system, and drastic action was needed. He said he was going to use a program recently approved by Congress, called the Troubled Asset Relief Program or "TARP," to buy lots of stock in each of their banks. He said that public confidence would be restored in their banks if they knew the government was standing behind them. He also said that the Federal Reserve would be willing to lend their banks lots of money and that the FDIC would temporarily guarantee their debt to make sure they could continue borrowing money to keep operating.

Ben spoke after Hank, reinforcing his order to the banks that they *had* to take the government's money. In a meeting held in Hank's office a few hours earlier, I had been surprised to learn that Hank and Ben were going to force these banks to accept the government's TARP money. Most of them, I thought, were healthy enough to get through the crisis without much government help, but some, like Citi, were in deep trouble and needed a lot of government assistance. Hank was worried that if the government just invested in Citi, it would make Citi's problems even worse by sending a signal that Citi had bigger problems than the others.

At Hank's request I explained our debt guarantee program. A few weeks earlier, at Tim's instigation,

Hank and Ben had asked me to announce that the FDIC was going to stand behind all obligations of the $13 trillion banking system. I told them no—we did not have the resources to make such a promise, even if I thought it was a good idea, which I didn't. Instead, we developed an alternative program to guarantee only new debt that these banks needed to issue to replace debt that was expiring. That was the program I was explaining. (We ended up insuring only about $300 billion in bank debt. Fortunately, we did not suffer major losses on the program and ending up collecting about $12 billion in fee income.)

Hank then asked Tim to tell each bank how much capital it would accept from the Treasury. He ticked down the list: $25 billion each for Citigroup, Wells Fargo, and JPM Chase; $15 billion for Bank of America; $10 billion each for Merrill Lynch, Goldman Sachs, and Morgan Stanley; $3 billion for Bank of New York; and $2 billion for State Street.

Then the questions began.

John Thain wanted to know if the government was going to limit his compensation if Merrill Lynch took the money. I couldn't believe it. His investment bank was in deep trouble, taxpayers were going to have to take huge risks to help him, and he was worried about his pay! (Months later, Thain would lose his job at Merrill over his payment of excessive bonuses to Merrill executives and lavish, million-dollar office renovations.) To his credit, Lewis said he didn't think they should be discussing their pay. I was then surprised to hear someone ask whether they could use the FDIC's debt guarantee program without taking the TARP money. I thought Tim was going to levitate out of his chair. "No," he almost shouted. It was like to his mind, we were competing with one another over which bailout program the banks would like the most! Vikram Pandit was busy scribbling numbers on the back of an envelope. Then he stopped and said, "This is cheap capital." I wondered what kind of math it took to figure that out. Nobody other than the government was willing to invest in Citi. For that bank any capital was going to be cheap.

Kovacevich complained that his bank didn't need the $25 billion. My jaw dropped when I heard Hank say that Wells's regulator might have something to say about that. Dimon, whose bank at that point was probably the healthiest of the group, tried to calm things down by saying that Chase would take the money even if it didn't need it, if that's what the government wanted. Blankfein and Mack said much the same thing.

All of the banks, even Wells, ended up taking the money. They all participated in the FDIC program too, which was a relief because if only the sick banks had participated, we would have had a real problem. We announced all the programs the next day in a big public press conference. When people first heard the news, they weren't sure what to think. The stock market actually went down. But as the news sunk in, the reaction was more positive. Investors became willing to lend money to banks again, and that was good for them.

So, there it was. The government of the United States—the bastion of free enterprise—had forcibly injected $125 billion into nine big banks, guaranteed hundreds of billions of their debt, and lent them trillions of dollars through the Federal Reserve. The financial system didn't fall apart, so we succeeded in something, I guess. But even with all that government help, those banks still pulled back on their lending to households and businesses (even as the smaller banks did a much better job providing credit to the economy). And the economy still suffered. People say that we "saved the system," but I don't take much pride in it. There is nothing heroic about throwing trillions of dollars of government money at big banks to keep them afloat.

In Part 1 I told you stories about the impact of the financial crisis on Main Street families. In Part 2 I would like to tell you my story. I served as chairman of the FDIC from June 2006 to July 2011. I want to tell you about our early efforts to try to stop bad mortgage-lending practices, to contain excessive risk taking by big financial institutions, and to try to help borrowers keep their homes. I want to tell you about the battles I won, the ones I lost, and the struggle being waged in Washington, DC, to reform our financial system, which continues to this day. I want to tell you about the unfairness of the bailouts and the terrible legacy of "too-big-to-fail." I want you to understand these problems because we have to get them fixed. The future of your generation depends on it.

CHAPTER 8
2006
THE END OF THE GOLDEN AGE OF BANKING

I became chairman of the Federal Deposit Insurance Corporation in June 2006. I was appointed to that job by President George H.W. Bush. My family and I—my husband, Scott; son, Preston; daughter, Colleen; and our two dogs, Cromwell and Pierre—had been living in Amherst, Massachusetts, where I taught at the university. Though we had lived in Amherst since 2002, my husband and I had spent most of our careers in Washington—him, working in the technology area and me, working in financial services.

I had already served one "tour of duty" with the Bush administration as the assistant secretary of the Treasury Department in 2001 and 2002. (I had also served in the president's father's administration from 1990 to 1995 as a commissioner at an agency called the Commodity Futures Trading Commission.) My job at the Treasury turned out to be a tough job with long hours as I helped handle the nation's response to the 9/11 terrorist attacks. One of the reasons Scott and I moved to Amherst was to have jobs that were less demanding so that we could have more time with our children.

I was a bit conflicted when the Bush administration asked me to come back, as we had a good, happy life in Amherst, an idyllic New England community. But I've always believed in public service, and I was very familiar with the FDIC, having worked with that agency closely when I was at the Treasury Department.

The FDIC was created in 1933 to prevent bank runs. During the Great Depression, households and businesses lost confidence in the banking system and started pulling their money out of the nation's banks en masse. Thousands of banks failed—even healthy ones—because they could not come up with all the cash necessary to meet withdrawal demands, having loaned out most of their deposits.

The collapse of the banking system had a terrible impact on the economy because there were not enough banks left to meet the borrowing needs of households and businesses. So Congress, during the administration of President Franklin Delano Roosevelt, created the FDIC to provide government insurance for deposits up to certain limits. In this way people knew that even if their bank got into trouble making bad loans or investments, the government would protect their money. And the agency has a perfect track record. Since its creation, no depositor has ever lost a penny, up to the deposit insurance limits. At the time that I took the FDIC job, our deposit insurance limit was $100,000. (Later, as a result of the crisis, Congress would raise it to $250,000.)

So I took the job leading this historic agency. Frankly, I thought it would be a 9-to-5 existence. No evening or weekend work, and certainly not the kind of intense pressure I experienced at the Treasury after 9/11. My children were still relatively young—Preston was twelve and Colleen was five—and it was important to me to have a job where I would have plenty of time with them. After all, we were in the "golden age of banking." Banks were healthy and experiencing record profits. No banks had failed in years.

In addition to protecting insured depositors, the FDIC also had responsibility for regulating thousands of small banks that were organized, or "chartered," by the states but qualified for FDIC insurance. The FDIC worked with state regulators to make sure that these banks were prudent in lending out money to depositors. But again, almost all those banks were making nice profits, so that job seemed quite manageable.

In fact, the banking sector had been so healthy and profitable for so long that most people in Washington had decided that regulation just wasn't that important anymore. This was a trend that had been ongoing since the 1990s, and one that I had resisted in the past. When I was a commissioner at the CFTC, for instance, I had opposed efforts to give broad regulatory exceptions for derivatives products (more about that later), and at the Treasury I had supported state and federal efforts to strengthen mortgage lending standards. But I had been out of the picture for four years while I was teaching at Amherst, and had no idea how pervasive this sense that financial firms didn't need regulation had become. The ravages of this deregulatory philosophy had particularly taken its toll at the FDIC.

For instance, the agency had undergone brutal layoffs. Its workforce had shrunk from 6,300 in 2001 to 4,500 by the time I arrived. As you might imagine, staff morale was terrible. The examination staff—the people who we sent to banks to make sure they were being responsible in their lending and other activities—had been cut significantly. The "Receivership and Resolutions" staff—the people who handled bank failures when they occurred—had been cut to the bone.

The FDIC staff were feeling overworked, and for good reason. Our economists and examiners were very concerned that housing prices would soon start to go down. They were also concerned that if people's homes lost value, they would start defaulting on their mortgages. Millions of people had subprime mortgages whose interest rates would be resetting to much higher rates in the next few years (like Matt's family in Part 1). If they couldn't refinance those mortgages because their homes had lost value, they would have to default, as they couldn't afford the higher rates. Though most of the smaller banks we regulated did not make subprime mortgages, they had made a lot of business loans that were tied to real estate. For instance, they made loans to contractors to build homes, or to build and operate shopping malls, restaurants, and other businesses that served housing developments. If homeowners started having trouble with their mortgages, eventually these commercial real estate loans would have trouble too.

It was hard for us to get a good picture of what was going on with mortgage lending because most of the high-risk loans—called subprime and "Alt-A"—were being put in securitizations and sold off to investors. The banks we insured had to file reports with us, but those reports only showed the loans that they made and kept on their books, not loans that were securitized. So we actually had to go out and buy that information. When we got it, we couldn't believe what we saw. These subprime mortgages had steep interest rate jumps— forcing payments up by a third or higher. And most of the borrowers barely made enough money to make the early payments, much less the higher resets. To make matters worse, if people refinanced their mortgages to avoid the resets, they would be charged a steep "prepayment penalty" that could be as high as 5% of the mortgage! These loans were like a volcano under the Pacific Ocean, out of sight and just waiting to erupt. Once they did, they would send a tidal wave of defaulting loans and lost homes onto our shores. Something had to be done—and done fast.

Unfortunately, I didn't have the power as the chairman of the FDIC to do much by myself. This is because financial regulation was—and still is—a hodgepodge of different regulators for different institutions, depending on where they are organized and whether they use FDIC-insured deposits. As I said, the FDIC regulated thousands of small, state-chartered banks, but most of them did not make subprime mortgages. Thrift institutions—specialty mortgage lenders—did make a lot of subprime and other risky mortgages. However, even though they used FDIC-insured deposits, they were regulated by another agency, the Office of Thrift Supervision, or "OTS." Big national banks also made subprime loans, but here again, while we insured their deposits, they were regulated by an agency called the Office of the Comptroller of the Currency, or "OCC." What's more, these big national banks didn't always make the subprime loans inside their OCC-regulated banks. Instead, they made them through a related institution, or "affiliate," that was regulated by yet another entity, the Federal Reserve Board. Finally, a majority of subprime mortgages weren't made by banks at all. Rather, they were being made by "mortgage bankers" that got their money through the securitization process and didn't use FDIC-insured deposits. Since they were not FDIC-insured banks and were not affiliated with insured banks, they weren't regulated by any of the federal bank regulators.

The only agency that had the power to write mortgage rules for everyone—banks and non-banks—was the Federal Reserve. For years, consumer groups and others had pleaded with the Federal Reserve to do so. When I was at the Treasury Department, I had worked with one of the Fed's own governors, Ned Gramlich, who tried to get the Fed to act, but the chairman at the time, Alan Greenspan, and the Fed's powerful staff flatly refused. They believed that it was better to let the industry regulate itself. In 2006 that was still the prevailing view at the Fed.

So we decided to at least try to get all four federal bank regulators—us, the OTS, the OCC, and the Fed—to tighten lending standards for banks the FDIC insured. When I arrived at the FDIC, the bank regulators were already working on new standards for what they called "nontraditional mortgages," or "NTMs." These were crazy mortgages that actually got more, not less expensive, as you paid them off. That is because for the first few years of the loan you could pick the payment you wanted to make, and it might be so small that it wouldn't even cover the interest on the mortgage. So each month the unpaid interest would be added to the principal balance, making it bigger and bigger. The problem was that eventually the borrower had to start repaying the principal, too. And like subprime loans, these loans had steep interest rate resets on them. Instead of calling these loans "NTMs," we should have called them "TNTs" because of the way their payments would explode in the faces of homeowners after a few years.

The bank regulators were working on new standards that required banks and thrifts to make sure the borrower had enough income to cover not only the early payments, which were lower, but also the higher payments that would come due later on. That was just common sense, but that wasn't the practice of thrift institutions. They were primarily looking at whether the borrower could make the early, lower payments. So the OTS objected to these standards! You would have thought that the OTS would be worried about so many thrift customers getting these exploding loans. But thrifts were making big money off them, because borrowers would always have to refinance them before the payments exploded. That generated another round of fees for the thrifts. It seemed like the OTS was more interested in protecting its thrifts than it was in protecting its thrifts' customers.

I objected to the new standards but for a different reason. They weren't strong enough since they didn't apply to subprime loans. The OCC had cleverly drafted the standards to exclude subprime loans with their exploding interest rate resets. I suspected that was because the OCC's national banks did not make NTMs, though they did make subprime loans. My view was that all borrowers should be protected from mortgages that had exploding payments, and that banks and thrifts should be required to make sure their borrowers could afford the mortgage throughout the life of the loan. The OCC supported applying that kind of principle to the NTMs that thrifts made, but did not want to apply it to subprime loans, which its own national banks made.

This was just one of many ways I would learn that bank regulators would negotiate and maneuver to protect their banks. We were playing childish games, trying to write rules not to protect the public but to give one particular group of institutions an advantage over another. This was like the NFL trying to rewrite the rules for professional football to say that the AFC teams only got three points for their touchdowns, while NFC teams got six. The OCC also went after smaller banks (which the FDIC mostly regulated) in discussions over commercial real estate lending. Again, the OCC was pushing for standards that would help big national banks but hurt the community banks with whom those big banks competed.

Here is what was going on. As I mentioned earlier, thousands of community banks specialize in commercial lending to small local businesses and builders. Many of these loans are made to build or buy commercial buildings—office buildings, shopping malls, hotels, restaurants, apartments. Or they are made to contractors to build new housing developments. These kinds of loans are called commercial real estate loans, or "CRE," and they are the bread and butter of most community banks' business.

The OCC wanted new standards that limited the dollar amount of CRE lending a bank could make to 300% of its capital. So let's say a community bank had $100 million, and $90 million of that came from deposits and $10 million came from capital investment from its shareholders. Under this rule the community bank could make only $30 million in CRE loans.

The OCC was clever to focus on whether a bank had most of its loans concentrated in CRE lending, instead of focusing on the quality of those loans. When we negotiated mortgage standards, we didn't talk about whether a bank or thrift had a concentration in mortgages—we focused on standards to make sure the borrower could repay. To be sure, there were risks with CRE loans. Some were being made without enough attention to whether the borrower would be able to pay the loan back. But that was true with both big banks and small banks. However, by focusing on concentrations, not the borrower's ability to repay the loan, these new standards hurt small banks' ability to make these loans—even good ones if they went over the cap—while leaving the big banks to do what they wanted.

The battles over mortgage lending standards and CRE lending were awful, but by far the toughest—and nastiest—battle was over bank capital standards. As discussed in Part 1, homeowners were not the only ones

who took on too much debt leading up to the crisis. Big banks did as well. Unfortunately, both the Fed and the OCC were pressuring the FDIC to change our rules so big banks could borrow even more! A group of international regulators had agreed to new rules that basically let big banks borrow as much as they wanted. These rules were called "Basel II" after the city in Switzerland where the regulators met. They had adopted Basel II in Europe, and big banks were really increasing their borrowing. Indeed, some banks were borrowing $50 for every $1 of equity capital contributed by its shareholders, or "owners." Think of that! It would be kind of like your parents borrowing 50 times more than the value of everything your family owns, including your house and all your savings accounts. Most families would view that much borrowing as way too much, and they would be right.

BANK CAPITAL RULES AND WHY THEY ARE IMPORTANT

Regulators try to keep large financial institutions from borrowing too much by making them raise a certain minimum portion of money for their business with common equity. There are two basic ways a financial institution or any other kind of company can raise money. It can issue what is called "equity," which is basically a way to sell little pieces of itself off

to investors. These investors are called "shareholders," and by buying equity, also known as "stock" or "shares," they essentially own a tiny bit of the bank or company. The other way of raising money is through borrowing. They can borrow by issuing "bonds," a kind of IOU that investors buy. They can take out loans from other financial institutions. Or they can take your deposits. Yes, deposits are a kind of borrowing. When you deposit money in a bank, you are essentially lending your money to it temporarily.

Bank regulators restrict a big bank's borrowing by requiring that a certain minimum percentage of its money comes from shareholders. These minimums are called "capital requirements." Regulators want banks to have lots of equity capital because it is "loss absorbing." For instance, if a big financial institution raises 10% of its money from shareholders, and 90% from borrowing, it can lose up to 10% of its money and still be solvent. That's because it has no legal obligation to pay back that 10%. Shareholders make money when an institution does well, but they lose money when it does poorly.

In contrast, when an institution borrows money, there is a legal obligation to pay that money back, regardless of how well the institution is doing. If financial institutions can't pay back their debts, they

"fail." Unfortunately, prior to the crisis, because of the Basel II rules, many big financial institutions were getting only about 2% or 3% of their money from shareholders; the rest was coming from borrowing. They could lose only 2% to 3% of their money before they would fail. And for many, losses were much bigger than 2% to 3%!

We thought it was nuts for big banks to be operating with so much borrowed money and wanted to stop these rules in the US. But the other regulators—both in the US and Europe—thought that big banks knew how to manage their risks better than the government. If the big banks felt it was safe for them to operate with that much borrowed money, the regulators shouldn't second-guess.

Part of my job as FDIC chairman was to attend the meetings of the international group called the "Basel Committee" that had written these bad capital rules. My first meeting with them was in Merida, Mexico. I remember the meeting like it was this morning. It was August and very hot, so I had on a sleeveless linen dress. Unfortunately, the hotel where we were meeting had the air-conditioning turned down to 60 degrees. I was trying so hard not to shiver because I didn't want these other regulators to think I was scared of them.

I made all my arguments—good arguments, obvious arguments—about how we needed to limit big-bank borrowing, but they all ganged up on me. I was like the new kid in class. They didn't think a newcomer should be telling them what to do.

So they refused to tighten the rules. In Europe, the big banks kept borrowing excessively, and in the US, big investment banks—which did not use FDIC insurance—also used these new rules to start borrowing more. We did stop the new rules for FDIC-backed banks (thank goodness), but we had to fight several more ugly battles over the issue.

All this haggling was already going on when I got to the FDIC, and these kinds of childish, inter-agency battles continued throughout my five years there, even after the terrible financial crisis, I am sad to say. We did finally get the OCC and OTS to agree to tougher mortgage lending standards for both subprime mortgages and NTMs, but it was not until the summer of 2007 that we finished that work. By then it was too late—so much of the damage had been done. So we refocused our efforts to convince banks and securitization investors to go back and change, or "restructure," all the bad loans that had already been made.

CHAPTER 9

2007

STEPPING OVER A DOLLAR
TO PICK UP A NICKEL

Our efforts to strengthen subprime lending standards met with a lot of opposition from the industry. I remember well a meeting I had in January 2007 with a big group of mortgage lenders. They had requested the meeting to try to convince me that tougher standards weren't needed. This kind of "lobbying" of regulators unfortunately goes on all the time. When I asked them about rising delinquencies on subprime loans, they said there was nothing wrong with the mortgages they made. It was all the borrowers' fault. They said borrowers just didn't care about repaying their mortgages. Then after criticizing borrowers, they shifted gears a bit and said that tougher standards would hurt borrowers because it would be harder to get mortgages.

This argument made me angry. It was a lie. In truth, fixed-rate mortgages—those without exploding payments—were available to subprime borrowers and were cheaper than the exploding variety. The only reason for these exploding loans was to force borrowers to refinance and generate more fees.

I ignored these lobbyists, and we eventually finalized the standards, though the OCC continued to resist us. But those new standards weren't going to help the millions of borrowers who already had exploding loans and who would be unable to refinance because home prices were going down.

For them we basically had only one tool available to us: loan restructurings, also known as modifications.

As we discussed in Part 1, loan modifications are a time-tested tool used by lenders to lessen their losses when a borrower runs into trouble. If a lender has to foreclose on a loan, the losses are usually quite substantial. If as an alternative, a lender can reduce the payment to make it affordable for the borrower and avoid foreclosure, that will save the lender money.

So why wouldn't lenders just restructure the loans on their own, since it would make financial sense for them to do so? Why did the government need to do anything?

In a word, securitization.

WHY IN THE WORLD DID SO MANY INVESTORS BUY SECURITIES BACKED BY BAD MORTGAGES?

One thing that has always mystified me: If it was so easy for us at the FDIC to find out about all the bad loans in these pools of mortgages, why weren't investors also seeing these problems? Why did they keep buying securities that were backed by these mortgages when it was so obvious that a big percentage of the borrowers couldn't pay them back?

I think there were two reasons.

One, instead of doing their own homework on these securitizations, they relied on other companies to do that homework. These companies are called "ratings agencies." Their job was to look at the loans inside the securitization pools and figure out how likely it was that some of the loans would default and cause losses for investors. In other words, their job was to grade, or "rate," the loans, kind of in the way your teacher might rate or grade how well you do on a test. But they were very sloppy in doing this work. Instead of looking closely at each of the loans, they relied on the fact that in the past, borrowers didn't usually default on their mortgages. This would be like a teacher giving you a good grade on a test without really looking at your answers, simply because you did well on past tests. And of course, in the past, mortgage originators used better lending standards than they did once they could start selling loans to securitizers.

So credit rating agencies told investors these mortgage-backed securities were safe when they really weren't. They gave them what's called "triple A" grades, or ratings, when a lot of these securities really deserved "triple Fs." Some think these agencies were sloppy and ignored problems because the securitizers—the financial institutions wanting to sell these securities to investors—paid them a lot of money to rate the loans. This is what is called a "conflict of interest." Ratings agencies' jobs were to help investors decide whether to buy the securities that they rated. But the agencies were paid by securitizers who just wanted to make money selling the securities. The interests of the securitizers were in conflict with the interests of the investors. The ratings agencies were supposed to look after investors, but they were paid by the securitizers.

Second, though ratings agencies deserve a lot of the blame for what happened, investors also should bear some responsibility. If they had done a little more work, they would have been able to find out for themselves about the bad loans in these securitizations.

But they got greedy too. They saw all the money they could make on these securities, with their high interest rates, and so they bought them without asking too many questions.

Most of the troubled mortgages were in securitization trusts, as explained in Part 1. Investors owned them. The original lenders did not. And investors had different interests, because of the way the securitizations were set up. If a loan went into foreclosure, the losses would be severe. But only one group of investors would absorb those losses, those that held the "subordinate," or "first loss," securities. If, on the other hand, the loan was restructured to reduce the payment, then all the investors, including those holding the "senior" securities, would have to share the losses. In other words, it would be better for those senior security holders to foreclose, even though the losses were bigger, because somebody else would have to take the loss. And those senior securities holders were much more numerous and powerful than those who held the "first loss" securities.

The holders of the senior securities didn't care about maximizing profits for the entire trust. They just wanted to maximize their own profits, and the way to do that was to send homes into foreclosure and let the subordinate or "first loss" securities holders take all the losses.

At the FDIC we were very afraid that these same kinds of motives would drive a lot of mortgage-backed securities investors to oppose loan modifications. They would be happy to let loans go into foreclosure—even though that would be more costly—because the losses would fall to other investors. So in the spring of 2007 we called together a series of meetings with other government agencies, investors, securitizers, servicers, lawyers, accountants—all the people who were involved in organizing and investing in securitizations. We wanted everyone to try to reach agreement on modifying these loans en masse to keep people in their homes.

Our specific plan was to ask investors and securitizers to simply eliminate the interest rate resets on subprime mortgages. Just convert them into 30-year, fixed-rate loans, and keep them at the starter rate—which was already quite high—9% to 11%. Our research showed that most subprime borrowers would not be able to afford the higher, resetting rate. They would default. Borrowers simply couldn't afford them. So it wasn't like investors were giving up much. Almost everyone agreed, except for one man who represented investors in the senior securities. He was harshly critical of our proposal and even suggested that these senior investors should sue servicers if they tried to help people stay in their homes.

But almost everyone else did agree with us— including other investor representatives—so I thought we had a plan to move forward. I was delighted that they seemed to be putting the country's and home-owners' interests ahead of their own. Many of the people who participated in our meetings made public promises that these loans would be restructured. We didn't have the legal authority to force them to do so, but I naively thought that they wouldn't be making promises and public statements if they didn't plan on following through.

So we waited. Several months passed, and then in the fall of 2007 a mortgage expert named Mark Zandi did a survey to determine how many troubled subprime borrowers were getting loan modifications. Guess how many there were? Only 1%! I couldn't believe it. After all that work we did and all those promises, only 1% of subprime borrowers were getting any help.

I got angry and decided to start publicly criticizing the securitization industry for not doing more to help homeowners. I published an op-ed in the *New York Times* calling for widespread loan modifications of the kind we had pushed for in our meetings. I also went to New York to speak to a securitization group to challenge them on why they were not working to stop the rising tide of foreclosures. They almost booed me. One man raised his hand and said, "You can't help these people. If you give them a break, they will just take the money and go buy a flat-screen TV."

I couldn't believe it. This well-paid Wall Street guy was complaining about giving a subprime homeowner a break. I challenged him: "If you feel that way about 'these people,' why did you provide money for their mortgages to begin with?"

And do you know what he said to me?

"Bad regulation."

That's right. In January 2007 industry members were lobbying me against tougher regulation. But by October 2007, when I gave that speech and subprime loan defaults were rapidly escalating, the industry was blaming the problem on a failure to regulate.

My efforts to publicly embarrass the industry did get the attention of Treasury Secretary Hank Paulson. He decided to try to help us, gathering all the regulators together to put pressure on servicers—who were mainly regulated banks—to modify more loans. But we didn't have legal authority to force them to do so, since the loans were owned by investors, not the banks. And unfortunately, investors did not support our efforts.

We did finally get written, public commitments

for a specific program called the Hope Now Alliance. The servicers agreed to extend the starter rate on these exploding subprime loans for five years. It wasn't the permanent extension that I wanted, but it was better than nothing. But even that agreement was frequently breached. Servicers did not have enough staff to carry the program through, and their primary regulator—the OCC—did not force them to spend the money to do so. And investors continued to resist.

I will never forget attending a foreclosure prevention workshop in Southern California organized by Governor Arnold Schwarzenegger after we launched the Hope Now Alliance. (Yes, "the Terminator" was a big supporter of our efforts. Some in the press started calling him "the Modifier" because of his push to keep people in their homes through loan restructuring.) All of the big servicers were there. They set up booths where people were lined up to apply for loan modifications. I watched and listened as a nurse, with her elderly father in tow, presented all of her paperwork to the servicer representative. The nurse had never been late on her mortgage, but she had an exploding subprime loan and couldn't afford the higher payments. The servicer gave her a loan modification but only for two years! I couldn't believe it. She was exactly the kind of borrower we wanted to help. Hardworking. Honest. Always on time with her mortgage. I called the head of the servicer when I returned to my office in Washington and complained loudly, but he said that they needed investor approval to modify loans, and their investors would only agree to two-year extensions.

I had many seasoned FDIC staff working for me who had decades of experience in restructuring loans for troubled borrowers as part of the agency's work in cleaning up failed banks. I was devastated at our inability to convince the Wall Street securitization industry to eliminate these "exploding" high interest rates, when it was so obvious the vast majority of borrowers could not afford them. "These guys will step over a dollar to pick up a nickel," one of our most experienced staffers told me.

In other words, they were so greedy, they didn't want to give up any money to troubled borrowers, even if by doing so, it would prevent later defaults and save money. They didn't care about the broader interests of homeowners and our economy. Like spoiled children, they wanted to keep what was theirs.

CHAPTER 10

2008

BAILING OUT
THE BLOCKHEADS

By the end of 2007 the number of homeowners who were late on their subprime mortgages had risen significantly. The foreclosure rate had more than doubled from the year before. By early 2008 the country was slipping into "recession," meaning that the economy was actually shrinking, not growing. Despite these warning signs, the Fed and the Treasury Department kept saying that subprime was "contained." In other words, they felt that problems with subprime mortgages would not spill over and hurt the broader economy. But that was already happening.

Citigroup, in particular, was starting to have problems. It lost $9.8 billion in the last three months of 2007, and lost another $5.1 billion in the first three months of 2008. Even still, the New York Fed and OCC, its primary regulators, kept letting Citi pay out big amounts of money—"dividends"—to its shareholders, money that Citi should have been keeping to handle all of its losses. In both 2007 and 2008, Citi was one of the biggest dividend payers in the country—not just among other banks but among all companies.

Citi was also making bad management decisions. In late 2007, Citi replaced its head since 2003, a man named Chuck Prince. Prince had been Citi's top lawyer—a very smart man—but not experienced in running a bank. Prince was replaced with Vikram Pandit. Pandit also had no commercial banking experience. He was a hedge fund manager, and not a successful one at that. Earlier that year Citi had bought the hedge fund that Pandit managed for $800 million. Pandit had personally reaped $165 million out of the deal. The hedge fund was performing so poorly that less than a year later Citi had to close it! And now they were making him the head of the bank.

The real reason, I suspected, was that Bob Rubin wanted Pandit to have the job, and Bob Rubin was close to Citi's most important regulator, Tim Geithner, who then headed the New York Fed. Citi wanted to keep Rubin happy because they needed to keep Geithner happy. These decisions, I felt, were all being made based on personal relationships. No one was thinking about what was best for the management of the bank.

I regret now that in early 2008 I wasn't paying more attention to Citi. But at that point I still assumed that Citi's regulators—the New York Fed and OCC—knew what they were doing. What's more, the FDIC didn't have a huge exposure to Citi. Citi only had about $125 billion in insured deposits and about $2 trillion in assets. Since the FDIC is entitled to seize a bank's assets to cover its losses, if the unthinkable happened and Citi did fail, its assets would have been more than ample to cover any FDIC losses.

I had more immediate problems. A number of thrift institutions that had made a lot of subprime and other risky loans on the West Coast were in deep trouble. Though housing prices were falling throughout the country, the declines were worse in previously "hot" real estate markets like California. More and more people were falling behind on their mortgages, and many were losing their homes to foreclosure. Losses on these mortgages were growing rapidly. Independent subprime lenders (those that were not banks and did not use insured deposits) were all going into bankruptcy. The three biggest thrifts were all having serious problems, and I did not have confidence in their regulator, the OTS.

Two of those three—Countrywide and Golden West—were already in the process of selling themselves to national banks. Countrywide would eventually be sold to Bank of America, and Golden West to Wachovia. (These overpriced sales would create big problems for the acquirers later on.) But the third, Washington Mutual, or WaMu, did not want to sell itself, even though it was in desperate need of money. It wanted to remain independent, and I suspected that its regulator, the OTS, was also discouraging it from selling itself. With the Countrywide and Golden West sales to national banks regulated by the OCC, the OTS would lose two of the three biggest institutions that it regulated. It did not want to lose WaMu, too.

WaMu's problems became more severe after a midsize investment bank called Bear Stearns was sold in a "forced marriage" to JPM Chase. Bear ran a hedge fund that had invested heavily in complicated securities and derivatives that were tied to subprime mortgages. For reasons that remain unclear to me, Tim Geithner forced the firm to sell itself to JPM Chase and even provided government assistance to Chase to buy it. It was not apparent that Bear's bankruptcy would have caused problems for the economy, and many people (including me) feel that this early government bailout created expectations that the government would protect other Wall Street firms from losses. This was a harmful expectation, as it discouraged these firms from taking steps of their own to raise more capital and sell bad investments (as was the case with Lehman Brothers, discussed below). It reinforced the notion that some institutions were too big to fail. And Bear wasn't even that big!

In any event, after the Bear sale, investors started looking more closely at other financial institutions that had invested heavily in subprime mortgages, and WaMu didn't look too good. Fresh off its government-assisted purchase of Bear, JPM Chase let it be known that it was interested in buying WaMu, too. Jamie Dimon, the charismatic head of Chase, made courtesy visits to me, Bernanke, and Paulson, with detailed analysis showing that WaMu had huge numbers of "exploding" mortgages that were likely to default. He wasn't looking for government assistance to buy WaMu, but I do think he was hoping that the government would put pressure on it to sell.

The OTS, of course, was resisting. OTS examiners insisted that the thrift was in relatively good shape. Our examiners thought otherwise. We thought WaMu needed to sell, or at least raise a lot more capital from investors to absorb huge mortgage losses. We were told that, with the OTS's blessing, WaMu wouldn't even talk with Chase. I weighed in with John Reich, the head of OTS, and told him emphatically that the WaMu board needed to consider all of its options, including Chase's offer to buy WaMu for $8 a share.

The WaMu board did not accept the Chase offer. Instead, WaMu raised more capital by issuing $7 billion to private investors. These private investors were friendly to WaMu's current management team and agreed to let them keep their jobs. If they had sold to Chase, they would have likely been replaced.

We were skeptical that $7 billion would be enough to absorb all of WaMu's losses. It was small compared to WaMu's $300 billion in assets, most of which were risky mortgage loans. But for a time, at least, the new capital seemed to give confidence to WaMu's creditors, and they kept lending it money. But by the late summer of 2008, WaMu was starting to have trouble again—big trouble.

It started in mid-July, after a much smaller thrift lender called IndyMac failed. Like WaMu, IndyMac had made a lot of risky loans on the West Coast. IndyMac's failure renewed worries about WaMu. WaMu's uninsured depositors—those people and businesses who had more than $100,000 on deposit with it—were starting to pull their money out. They were worried that if WaMu failed, they would lose part or all of these uninsured deposits.

In late July the head of WaMu—a man named Kerry Killinger—called me and asked me for help. I told him, truthfully, that there wasn't anything I could do. I told him that he needed to sell his bank or raise a lot more capital. And I reminded him that if WaMu failed, our process was a harsh one, just like bankruptcy. His shareholders would lose all of their money, and he and his management team would lose their jobs.

That clearly wasn't the response he was looking for. A few days later John Reich called me and asked me to attend a meeting in his office to get a briefing about WaMu. I went to the meeting and took some of my top staff with me. We listened politely as Killinger and other WaMu executives told us that they were just fine. They acknowledged that their mortgages would have big losses, but said they would make plenty of money to cover those losses. In making that statement, they unrealistically assumed that the economy would grow and be healthy, even though we were already in the middle of a bad recession. We told them, again, that they either needed to raise a lot more capital or sell themselves. John Reich angrily cut us off and later sent an e-mail to his staff that he could not believe "the audacity of that woman." "That woman" was, of course, me.

We stepped up pressure on WaMu and the OTS and finally got them to try to find a buyer, but it was too late. Uninsured depositors were withdrawing $3 billion a day. On September 25, 2008, the OTS ended up having to close the thrift before it ran out of money. We auctioned it off and JPM Chase was, by far, the highest bidder. WaMu's shareholders were wiped out, and its board and management all lost their jobs. If only the OTS had spent as much time regulating WaMu as it had fighting us, we might have been able to prevent that failure. If WaMu had sold itself to Chase that spring, its shareholders would not have lost all of their money.

Fortunately for us, our process for handling failed banks was a smooth one. The transfer to Chase was seamless. Much to my surprise, the failure barely received any press coverage. We were actually feeling pretty confident at the FDIC about our ability to handle further failures. We were stretched, but we had been planning for these problems, and we had the tools and expertise to deal with failing banks. Throughout its history the FDIC has smoothly handled thousands of bank failures. That is what it was established to do.

Outside of FDIC-insured banks in the so-called "shadow" sector, however, all heck was breaking loose. On September 7 the government had taken over Fannie Mae and Freddie Mac—two entities created by Congress to support the housing market. Fannie and

Freddie had invested heavily in subprime mortgage-backed securities, mostly with borrowed money. Rapidly increasing losses on those investments caused them to become insolvent.

FANNIE MAE IS NOT A CANDY

The kinds of securitizations that generated so many unaffordable mortgages in the lead-up to the subprime crisis were called "private label" securitizations. They were put together by large financial institutions, many of which had not been involved in mortgage lending before. However, decades ago the federal government had created special companies called "government-sponsored enterprises," or "GSEs" for short, whose job it was to support mortgage lending for middle-income households. These entities were called the Federal National Mortgage Association, commonly referred to as "Fannie Mae," and the Federal Home Loan Mortgage Association, or "Freddie Mac."

These two companies bought mortgages from banks and other lenders if the loan amount was below a certain limit. This limit—called the conforming loan limit—was meant to cover the amount a typical middle-income family might borrow to buy a house, but not to cover houses purchased by wealthier people. Just like a "private label" securitizer, Fannie and Freddie would pool these mortgages together and sell off interests in them to investors. However, unlike private label securitizers, Fannie and Freddie would guarantee the mortgage payments. If a borrower defaulted—that is, stopped paying back the mortgage—Fannie and Freddie would step in and make up the difference. Fannie and Freddie charged a fee for providing this guarantee. Because Fannie and Freddie had to step in if borrowers defaulted on their mortgages, they were both pretty careful about the loans they securitized. In fact, while investors suffered losses on 20% of all loans securitized by "private label" issuers, Fannie and Freddie only suffered losses on about 4% of the loans they securitized and backed.

Unfortunately, Fannie and Freddie were not so careful when it came to investing their money. In addition to securitizing mortgages themselves, they were big purchasers of private label securities, and when those securities started to lose money, Fannie and Freddie lost money too. What's more, Fannie and Freddie, like a lot of large financial institutions, had their own huge debt obligations. In fact, over 97% of the money they used to support their investments was borrowed. Less than 3% came from their shareholders—the people who owned them and benefited from their big profits. When Fannie and Freddie started losing money on their private label mortgage-backed securities, they went broke. However, because they provided a lot of support to the housing market and the ability of middle-income people to get mortgages, the government took them over and continued their operations. But it cost the government a lot of money to keep them going. Taxpayers had to give Fannie and Freddie nearly $190 billion to keep them operating, but as of this writing in 2014, the GSEs are profitable again, and they are making money for taxpayers.

The next shoe to drop was Lehman Brothers, a $600-billion investment bank. It filed for bankruptcy on September 15. Lehman Brothers was twice the size of Bear Stearns, and it had also made a lot of stupid investments in securities and derivatives tied to risky mortgages. Everyone knew Lehman was in trouble, but I think its investors were expecting it to get a bailout, because Bear had gotten one and it was only half as big. The head of Lehman, a man named Dick Fuld, also assumed the government would bail him out, so he had turned down offers from other healthier institutions to buy his bank months earlier. But Hank Paulson decided against a bailout, so Lehman was forced into bankruptcy, and its shareholders and creditors took big losses.

Lehman was like the first domino to topple in a long line. (Did you know that the longest domino line to ever topple was 4,800,000 dominoes long? Sorry. I digress.) It spooked uninsured depositors at WaMu, accelerating WaMu's failure. Importantly, the Lehman, bankruptcy made investors think that there would be more failures. Many of these investors had bought something called credit default protection that would pay out if big financial institutions failed and defaulted on their debt. A lot of that protection, a kind of insurance, was sold by a big company called the American Insurance Group, or AIG. AIG's investors started worrying that it might also go bankrupt because it might have to pay out on all of that insurance if more financial institutions went into bankruptcy. So AIG started having trouble borrowing money to operate, and on September 16 the Fed started bailing it out with loans.

There was also a big fund called the Reserve Fund that had invested heavily in Lehman debt and took big losses on that debt when Lehman went bankrupt. The Reserve Fund was a special kind of fund called a "money market fund," which promises investors that every dollar they put in, they will get back, plus a little interest, just like a bank. The problem is that money market funds are not banks. They don't have deposit insurance, and they take people's money and sometimes invest it in risky places, even though they are not supposed to. That is what happened with the Reserve Fund. It took some of its investors' money and invested it in Lehman Brothers debt, assuming that the government would not let Lehman fail. But the government did let Lehman fail, and the Reserve Fund suffered big losses. As a result, it "broke the buck," meaning that families and businesses that had put their dollars into the fund would not get all of those dollars back. That then scared investors in other money market funds, and they all started pulling their money out of those other funds. Hank Paulson decided to bail out those funds with a temporary government insurance program. Taxpayers temporarily had to guarantee trillions in money fund investments.

Bear. AIG. Money market funds. Almost everyone was getting bailed out. And frankly, the Fed and the Treasury were making up a lot of these bailout programs. They had to. There was an established process for handling failures of FDIC-insured banks, but no "playbook" for these shadow banks, like investment banks, insurance companies, and money market funds. But Hank Paulson and Ben Bernanke were getting nervous that they were throwing around a lot of government money without Congress authorizing them to do so. They decided that they needed to go to Congress and ask them to authorize a bailout program that they called the "Troubled Asset Relief Program," or "TARP."

On September 20, Hank and Ben sent a request to Congress for $700 billion in bailout money. I think they would be the first to tell you that their original bill was not very well thought-out. It was basically a one-paragraph request for a lot of money. Congress said no. When Congress voted the bill down, investors became even more scared and started pulling money out of the stock market, which made stock prices go down. When Congress saw that happening, they realized they may have made a mistake. In addition, Hank had his staff work up a more detailed bill that did a better job of explaining how the Treasury Department was going to spend the money if Congress gave it to them. In particular, they promised that some of the money would be used to help homeowners avoid foreclosure. They also added a provision increasing deposit insurance limits to $250,000, which they felt would make it more popular with Main Street families like yours.

Hank and Ben kept talking with Congress, and it looked like they were going to get their TARP bill. The WaMu failure went smoothly, and it seemed like we might be able to work our way through this. But I soon discovered that the OCC and the Fed were not telling me everything that I needed to know. Citi's problems were becoming worse and worse. Unfortunately, behind my back, Tim Geithner at the New York Fed was concocting a plan to force me to give Citi a backdoor bailout.

On the evening of Friday, September 26, just a day after we sold WaMu to Chase, I got a call from John Dugan, the head of the OCC, saying that a national bank that he regulated, Wachovia, was having problems. This surprised me because we had been asking the OCC about Wachovia, and the OCC's examiners consistently said that it was okay. We had been worried about Wachovia because a year earlier it had purchased a West Coast thrift named Golden West. Golden West had made a lot of risky exploding mortgages, and after Wachovia had purchased it, they kept right on making them. Now a lot of those loans were going into default.

I was invited to participate in a conference call the next morning, Saturday, September 27, which was being hosted by Tim Geithner. And I did not understand why Tim Geithner was involved in the call, because Wachovia, being based in North Carolina, was overseen by the Richmond Federal Reserve Bank, not Geithner's New York Fed.

When the call started, I couldn't believe what I was hearing. OCC examiners were now saying that

Wachovia was likely to run out of cash if we didn't do something soon. Like WaMu, it was losing a lot of uninsured deposits. And then I heard why Tim Geithner was involved. He wanted the FDIC to help Citigroup buy Wachovia! I thought he was joking. I protested strongly. I had been told that Wells Fargo was interested in buying Wachovia and that, in fact, the heads of both banks were meeting that weekend to work out the terms of the purchase. I had heard that Wachovia was having problems—hence its decision to seek out a buyer—but no one had ever suggested that it was close to failure until then. In any event, it was best for the FDIC if Wells bought Wachovia without us having to get involved. Wells was a very strong bank. With its good management and strong finances, if it bought Wachovia, Wachovia would be fine.

The call ended with everyone agreeing that we should let the Wells and Wachovia discussions continue. But I was very worried that Tim had already been spreading it around that the FDIC might help Citi buy Wachovia, though that was the furthest thing from my mind. If word got out, Wells might pull out of the Wachovia discussions, thinking that it could get help from the FDIC, too. On Sunday, September 28, that is exactly what happened. Wells suddenly said that they wouldn't buy Wachovia without government help.

Wachovia's head, a man named Bob Steel, was livid. They had been very close to a deal. I was livid as well. I suspected that Tim had disrupted the negotiations with his loose talk about an FDIC-assisted deal for Citi. Now Wells wanted in on the action too.

With no prospect of a Wells purchase without our help, and the OCC's examiners saying that Wachovia might run out of money once it reopened on Monday, we had no other choice than to auction the bank off as we had done with WaMu. Thanks to Tim's shenanigans, I knew the FDIC would probably have to put money into the deal. Both Wells and Citi bid on the bank, and both wanted assistance. But Wells got greedy, and asked for a lot of help—much more than Citi wanted. Under our rules the sale goes to the best bidder, so we told Citi it could buy Wachovia. I was very upset with this result. I did not trust the New York Fed and the OCC when they said Citi was strong enough to buy Wachovia. But I had no way to challenge them under our process.

So we announced on Monday morning that Citi would buy Wachovia with government assistance. And guess what happened? Instead of working fast to finalize and sign all the contracts necessary to make the purchase, Citi started renegotiating the purchase with Wachovia, and didn't even tell us about it! On Wednesday, Citi still had not finalized the contracts to buy Wachovia. Then I was contacted by Dick Kovacevich, the head of Wells Fargo, who told me that Wells wanted to buy Wachovia after all, and he didn't want any help from the FDIC. He was offering $7 a share compared to the Citi offer of $1 a share. We were right back where we had been over the weekend until Tim had blown everything up with his talk about FDIC assistance. I told Kovacevich his offer was just fine with me, but that he needed to get signed contracts to Wachovia right away. That's exactly what he did, and not surprisingly, the Wachovia board jumped at the Wells offer. On Thursday morning Wells announced that they, not Citi, were going to buy Wachovia.

Tim Geithner blew a gasket. The Federal Reserve still had to approve Wells's purchase of Wachovia. All of the regulators had a big conference call on Friday. Tim argued that the FDIC should object to Wells's purchase. The FDIC had already publicly agreed to support Citi, he said, so it would look like the FDIC was going back on its promise. I told him that it was Citi's own fault for not getting all the contracts signed and trying to renegotiate the purchase. But that was typical, in my view, of Citi's weak management. They couldn't follow through on anything.

I also told Tim that if the Fed wanted to disapprove the Wells purchase, it had the legal authority to do so,

That's right. They would basically have me say that the FDIC was standing behind the entire $13 trillion banking system.

I told them we couldn't do that and wouldn't do that. It wasn't necessary. Banks that had lots of capital and that used insured deposits to support their operations weren't really having problems. I knew that Citi and the investment banks were having trouble because they didn't have a lot of capital and they borrowed money on a continuous basis from investors. Many of their loans had to be renewed daily. They were having a lot of trouble renewing their loans, but that was partly their own fault for relying so heavily on these very short-term loans.

I suspected Tim was behind this bold request and that Citi would be the primary beneficiary of such an action. But I was in a terrible spot. Here the secretary of the Treasury and the chairman of the Fed were basically telling me that the FDIC had to guarantee the entire banking system.

So I decided to give them a different proposal. We said we would temporarily guarantee new debt that these banks needed to issue to replace debt that was expiring, but that was all. So instead of backing the $13 trillion banking system, we ended up backing only about $300 billion in new debt. We also said we but the FDIC would have nothing to do with it. Of course, the Fed did not object. Tim wanted to use the FDIC to carry out his backdoor bailout of Citi. He was trying to get us to do something the Fed itself wouldn't do. I suspected that his plan all along was to get the FDIC to help Citi without looking like Citi needed help. But Citi needed help, and needed it badly. And Tim wasn't going to give up.

On October 8, Hank summoned me to a meeting in his office, but he wouldn't tell me what the meeting was about. When I arrived, Hank and Ben were sitting there next to a telephone. Tim Geithner was on the speaker. Hank told me to sit down and handed me a piece of paper. He said that the financial system was in big trouble and that the FDIC needed to publicly announce that it was going to back anyone who had lent money to the big banks. He, Ben, and Tim had even written up a little script for me to read at a press conference. It said:

"It is the policy of our federal government to use all resources at its disposal to make our financial system stronger. In light of current conditions, the FDIC, with the full support of the Fed and the Treasury, will use its authority and resources to protect depositors, protect unsecured claims, guarantee liabilities, and adopt other measures to support the banking system."

would charge a fee for our guarantee, and we wanted the healthy banks to participate to make sure we received plenty of fees. I didn't want to get stuck with just guaranteeing sick banks like Citi.

Ben and Hank readily agreed to this proposal, though Tim was against charging the banks more than nominal fees for our guarantee. We hammered out the details of the program over the weekend, along with a program the Treasury was going to launch with the TARP money that Congress finally gave it. Though the Treasury had originally asked Congress for the money to buy "troubled assets" from banks—to help them get rid of all the bad mortgage investments they had made—Hank changed his mind and decided instead to use $125 billion of the money to make capital investments in the largest banks. This was what they were doing in Europe, and it was going to be faster to just make investments in these banks instead of setting up a program to buy their troubled mortgages and mortgage securities.

Hank invited the heads of the nine biggest banks to come to a meeting on the following Monday, October 13. He, Ben, and Tim decided that they were going to order the banks to take the money, which surprised me because most of them, in my view, didn't need it. I suspected that this was partly to hide the fact that Citi was in trouble. If the government only bailed out Citi, everyone would know that it had serious problems.

All the banks agreed to do as they were told. The next morning we had a big meeting with President Bush to brief him on all of these bailout programs. He was very appreciative and went out of his way to thank me for the FDIC's debt guarantee program. His graciousness was a nice change after Tim's relentless bullying over the weekend. Shortly after our meeting with the president, we had a big press conference to announce these programs and that the nine biggest banks had agreed to participate in them.

The programs worked to help the banks. Investors were willing to lend them money again, and at very low rates, given all the government backing. But even though the whole purpose of these programs was to make sure the big banks kept lending to the economy, they didn't do a very good job. Their lending plummeted, and as a result, many responsible businesses and households could not borrow money that they needed to make purchases and investments. And even though I had insisted on making these banks promise to systematically modify mortgages to try to keep people in their homes, they didn't do much to help homeowners, either. Congress had specifically told Hank to use some of the TARP money for foreclosure prevention, but he never launched a program. He and his staff had some conversations with us, and we gave them detailed proposals for a program. But I just don't think their hearts were in it. Hank told me later that the new Obama administration informed him that they wanted to design their own foreclosure prevention program, so he decided to leave it to them.

Even though the programs we announced on October 14 were quite generous for the banks, they still weren't enough to help Citi. On Friday, November 21, I received a late-afternoon call from Hank notifying me that Citi was on the brink of collapse, and we needed to do another bailout. We spent the whole weekend in another round of calls on how much help Citi needed and how that help should be divided among the Treasury, Fed, and FDIC. The tension was eased a little bit when, during one of the calls, my daughter, Colleen—then eight—got on our extension at home to call her friend Katherine. We heard her punching the numbers and then heard her sweet little voice saying, "Hello?" "Colleen, Mommy's on the phone," I answered. She hung up, and after a three-beat pause, we all cracked up.

But for the most part the discussions were tense and ugly. Citi said it wanted the government to "ring-fence"—that is, agree to cover losses—on about $300 billion in mortgages, mortgage securities, and other loans and investments that were losing money. But Citi's leadership couldn't even identify precisely the loans and investments where it wanted the government to cover losses, so it was very hard for us to understand the risks they wanted us to take. The other problem was that Tim was insisting that the FDIC take most of the risk in bailing out Citi. Like a schoolyard bully holding a grudge, he was still trying to pay me back for not supporting Citi's attempted purchase of Wachovia. I refused, given the relatively small amount of deposits the FDIC insured at Citi, and our ability to claim its assets to protect us from losses. At one point I even suggested that we should consider putting the FDIC-insured part of Citi into our bankruptcy-like process. That would have meant that Citi's board and executives would have lost their jobs, and their shareholders and creditors, not the government, would have had to cover the bank's losses. My suggestion certainly got a rise out of Tim and Hank. But in truth, I was bluffing. We couldn't proceed without the support and cooperation of Citi's primary regulators, the OCC and Tim's New York Fed. They had the information that we needed to close Citi in an orderly way. And they were adamant about doing a bailout.

So we ended up doing a second bailout of Citi, but the FDIC appropriately played only a small role. Hank decided to invest another $20 billion of TARP money into the bank, for a total investment of $45 billion. We agreed to cover only $10 billion in losses on $306 billion in ring-fenced loans and investments, with Citi, the Treasury, and the Fed taking the rest. The following Monday we announced the program. With that second bailout, taxpayers had invested $45 billion in Citi, the FDIC had guaranteed about $70 billion of its debt under our new program, the Fed had lent it tens of billions, and we had collectively agreed to cover its losses on over $300 billion of its assets. All of that, and Citi was still in trouble. A few months later, in February 2009, it would receive its third bailout.

THE VERY, VERY BAD DOCTRINE OF "TOO BIG TO FAIL"

When the government stepped in with taxpayer money to help big financial institutions who were in trouble, people got mad. Our economy is based on the notion of letting people and businesses take risks to produce goods and services, and letting them keep the profits if they succeed. But if they make mistakes and lose money, they are supposed to suffer the consequences, and not make the rest of us share in their problems. These big financial institutions' shareholders—the investors who owned them—and the executives who ran the companies had made many billions of dollars in profits from securitizing mortgages and making derivatives bets on the direction of the mortgage markets. Their creditors—that is, the people and firms who had lent them money—also made profits off the interest these big financial institutions paid on those borrowings. But the government protected them, so they were able to keep their profits while putting the risk of losses on the government when things got bad.

What is the doctrine of "too big to fail"? Very simply, it is the idea that you can lend a large financial institution lots of money, and you don't have to worry about losing any of that money because if the big financial institution gets into trouble, the government will pay you back. That is, the government will bail you out. This is a very dangerous idea, and let me tell you why.

Let's suppose you have a very rich uncle—we will call him "Sam." Say your uncle Sam tells all of your friends that you are his very favorite niece or nephew, and because he likes you so much, they can lend you all the money they want, with interest, and if you have any trouble paying them back, he will pay them off himself. Now, what do you think your friends would do? They would be happy to lend you lots of money, and get that interest, because there is no risk they will lose with your rich uncle backing you up. They won't ask you any questions about what you are going to use the money for, or where you will get the money to repay them. They don't care, knowing your uncle Sam is there to protect them.

And how would this guarantee from your uncle affect your behavior? You would probably start borrowing lots of money since your friends would be so eager to lend it to you. They would probably even compete with one another to make loans to you, which means you probably wouldn't have to pay them a lot of interest. And being able to borrow so cheaply and easily, you would probably decide not to use your own money to buy things, but rather use borrowed money to buy that new iPhone you have been wanting, or maybe a big flat-screen TV for your room. Why use your own money when your friends are so eager to lend to you?

The idea of "too big to fail" had somewhat the same impact on big financial institutions prior to the crisis, though the government guarantee they enjoyed was implicit, not explicit like your uncle Sam's. That is, many investors assumed that the government would bail them out because they were so big and important to our economy, even though the government never came out and actually said it would do so. In fact, this assumption was so pervasive that credit rating agencies (discussed above) actually gave the debt of big banks higher ratings because of it. With this implicit government backing, lots of financial institutions went out and borrowed a lot of money, and they weren't very careful with how they used it, because investors, and bondholders in particular, were not asking them many questions. They took big risks with their money, and that is why they got into trouble. And when we bailed them out with government programs in 2008 and 2009, what investors assumed to be implicit then became explicit.

"Too big to fail" is so dangerous because it encourages financial institutions to take big risks with borrowed money. If the big risks pay off, they will make a lot of money. If they don't work out, the government will come to the rescue. Many people (including me) think that "too big to fail" is morally wrong because it gives big financial institutions protection from their own mistakes, a benefit that the rest of us don't enjoy. But more than being wrong, the idea is bad economics. It makes our financial system less stable because it encourages big financial institutions to take lots of risks. If bondholders and others who lent them money asked more questions of them and refused to lend to them if they were taking too many risks, this would force more discipline on their behavior. Otherwise, they wouldn't be able to borrow. But this kind of discipline—called "market discipline"—is absent with "too big to fail."

CHAPTER 11

2009

THE MORE THINGS CHANGE, THE MORE THEY STAY THE SAME

The year 2009 brought with it a new president, Barack Obama. I was desperately hoping that the new administration would rethink some of the bailout policies we were pursuing and would do more to help distressed homeowners. Unfortunately, that was not to be. President Obama promised to launch stronger programs to prevent foreclosures, and I really think that helping these families was a priority for him. But I do not believe that the people he picked for major economic positions in his administration shared those priorities.

Much to my surprise and disappointment, he

picked Tim Geithner to replace Hank Paulson as the new secretary of the Treasury. Throughout the crisis, Tim's singular focus had been to bail out the big banks, and in particular, Citi. He had shown little interest in foreclosure prevention or any other kind of direct help for Main Street. He viewed the big banks as the center of our economy, and equated helping them with helping the broader economy. He did not understand that their interests and Main Street interests were separate, and that helping big banks did not necessarily help struggling American families.

President Obama also picked Larry Summers, another close associate of Bob Rubin, to head the National Economic Council, or "NEC," which was responsible for developing economic policy for the White House. Summers had also once served as secretary of the Treasury and had been a supporter of legislation to block regulation of the derivatives markets. In addition, he had backed legislation to repeal a Depression-era law called "Glass-Steagall," which for decades had prohibited FDIC-insured banks from engaging in risky securities activities. Based on Summers's record, I also viewed him as highly sympathetic to the big banks.

The first few months of the new administration were rough for me. Shortly after Obama announced his decision to nominate Tim as the new Treasury secretary, it was leaked to the press that Geithner was trying to force me out of my job, even though I had a fixed, five-year term that would not expire until 2011. Important members of Congress wrote to the president strongly supporting me, and the president ended up essentially announcing on television that he wanted me to stay. I was flattered that the president so publicly announced his respect for me. Needless to say, though, I was embarrassed by press reports that Tim wanted me fired.

But Tim was also having a rough time. His appointment to be Treasury secretary had to be approved, or "confirmed," by the Senate, and many members opposed him because of his bailout policies. They were also concerned that he had failed to pay all of his taxes—quite a problem for the man who would lead the department charged with making sure people paid their taxes! But he was eventually confirmed, and some of his early initiatives (much to my pleasant surprise) were positive. His first priority was to make a public announcement that any bank over $100 billion would be subject to a "stress test" by regulators to make sure it had enough capital to stay solvent if the economy got a lot worse (and the economy was pretty bad already). He also wanted to launch a program to buy banks' troubled assets—the original idea behind the TARP law.

I was strongly supportive of a "troubled asset" program that would force the largest banks to get rid of the bad loans and investments they had made. This would enable the government to tackle restructuring the mortgages to make them affordable for honest families who desperately wanted to keep their homes. For instance, the idea was for the government, working in partnership with private investors, to buy distressed mortgages at discounts. So, for example, an "exploding" mortgage with an unpaid loan amount of $150,000 might be purchased for $100,000. As the new owner of the loan, the government could convert it into a 30-year fixed-rate mortgage, and even reduce the loan amount. The loan amount could be reduced to, say, $125,000 to make it more affordable for the borrower, but the government would still make $25,000 over its purchase price of $100,000.

I also did not oppose the stress test idea because I thought this would be a good way to force banks to raise more capital. The biggest banks were not doing their jobs lending into the economy, and the best way to get them lending again was to force them to get rid of all their bad assets—a process called "cleaning up the balance sheet"—and build a bigger capital base. The reason many of them were not lending was because they knew they were going to have a lot more losses from bad loans and investments, and they were worried that they didn't have enough capital to absorb those losses. So they were playing it safe, and not taking additional risks by making new loans.

So Tim had some good ideas, but he also had some bad ones. He wanted to announce that any bank that failed its stress test would get government capital from TARP. In other words, he was going to bail out any bank with assets more than $100 billion. I thought this was terribly unfair to the smaller banks. When regulators determined that these banks were insolvent, they were put into the FDIC's bankruptcy-like process. Taxpayers did not bail them out. Their managers lost their jobs, and the banks were sold to either healthier banks or investor groups who were willing to strengthen the bank with new capital. The FDIC had used this process thousands of times, and it was the fastest way to clean up a failed bank and get it lending into the economy again. Many people, including legendary investor Warren Buffett, criticized Tim's new bailout plan, saying point-blank that Citi's problems were tainting the entire banking industry. He said (and I agreed) that even if these other banks failed their stress tests (unlikely because most were healthy), the FDIC could easily handle them with our process.

So the initial public reaction to Tim's plans was controversial, but he was the new Treasury secretary, backed by the president, and I had no place to turn for help with my concerns. So I reluctantly agreed to participate, assuming that we would at least launch the troubled asset program to force banks to sell their bad assets. But even though Tim announced this plan, and I strongly supported it, he would never follow through with it. I am guessing that he finally realized that the banks would have to absorb big losses if forced to clean up their balance sheets, and he just didn't want to make them do that. So we did the stress tests, and fortunately, almost all the banks that were found to need more capital were able to raise it from private sources so taxpayers did not have to bail them out. Citi was one of the few exceptions.

By February 2009, Citi was having problems again. Unbelievably, Tim was still after me, trying to pressure the FDIC into taking responsibility for most of Citi's bad assets. I told him no, again. The New York Fed and the OCC were Citi's primary regulators, but they kept trying to escape responsibility by dumping Citi onto the FDIC. I refused, and when I did, Tim decided to help them on his own by giving up the government's right to collect dividends on $25 billion of the $45 billion it had invested in Citi. Tim converted the government's "preferred shares" to "common shares," meaning that taxpayers no longer had a right to dividends. Unlike all the other big banks that received TARP money, Citi never did pay the government back on that $25-billion investment. Luckily, some time later, Tim was able to sell those common shares to other investors at a profit. In this way, taxpayers got their money back.

While Tim was primarily focused on the big banks and their needs, the president asked Larry Summers to come up with a foreclosure prevention program. The president had publicly talked about my efforts to help homeowners, so I think Larry felt obligated to talk with me as he began developing a foreclosure prevention program. But I got the impression that his heart just wasn't in it. He was just "checking the box" so he could tell the president that he had spoken to me.

My discussions with Larry started at the end of 2008 and continued into February 2009. I naively hoped that he was sincere in wanting some of our ideas. The FDIC had some of the government's best experts on securitization and modifying loans. We gave him detailed proposals and analysis. Unfortunately, the program he ended up presenting to the president was one we thought would not work, and we told him as much. He did adopt our approach for modifying loans, starting with reducing the interest rate, then lowering the principal amount. But his plan didn't provide powerful enough financial incentives for servicers and investors to do these modifications. And because the loans were in securitization trusts, the government couldn't force them to do so. He promised me that he would also pursue elements of our plan, which we thought had stronger incentives and a much better chance of working. But he never followed through on that promise, and the plan that they did pursue did very little to help homeowners. Years later I would learn of a memo that Larry had sent to the president in December 2008, rejecting our proposals. He had never taken our ideas seriously. I felt he had just led me on.

The president was eager to announce a program for protecting homeowners, and he asked me to go to Phoenix on February 18 to attend his speech about his home preservation efforts. I went, trusting Larry Summers's commitments to incorporate our ideas into their programs. In fact, as I boarded the plane for Phoenix, my staff were still in negotiations with Larry's team. In Phoenix the president gave a very powerful speech on behalf of homeowners. But as he started describing the programs Larry had given him, I cringed. He said that 3 to 4 million borrowers would be helped under the program, which was wildly optimistic given the program's basic flaws. In fact, two years later only about half a million homeowners had actually been helped.

On the trip back to Washington from Phoenix, the president asked me to ride with him on his plane, Air Force One. I was thrilled at the prospect of riding back with him. What a treat to ride on Air Force One! The area reserved for staff (where I rode, along with Tim and a number of White House aides) was furnished with overstuffed beige leather chairs and glossy wood tables. Paper place mats, napkins, and coasters—all embossed with the presidential seal—were scattered about, and yes, like a wide-eyed tourist, I stuffed a few in my purse.

About halfway back to Washington, I was settled in my overstuffed leather chair, sipping a Diet Coke and popping nuts out of a china bowl, when I heard the president's voice booming, "Sheila. What are you reading?" I looked up and saw him standing there. Everyone straightened up, casting jealous glances my way. "It's a book about risk," I answered. Which it was. Thank goodness I wasn't reading something frivolous like a Stephanie Plum novel. "Come with me," he said with a wave of his hand. I started to get up, then plopped right back down, forgetting that I had my seat belt on. On the second try I released the metal buckle, successfully rose from my chair, and followed him to his office, a spacious room near the front of the plane.

We must have talked a good twenty to thirty minutes. He was full of questions about the banking system, and wanted my frontline view from the FDIC. We talked at length about homeowners facing foreclosure, as well as the problems that families and small businesses were having getting loans. I felt that he really cared about Main Street families, and didn't give a hoot about the big banks. I also felt that he sincerely wanted to hear my perspective, unlike the "check the box" conversations I had had with Larry.

The loan modification program the president announced that day never did much good, and I think that was because it was designed by people who just felt obligated to have some kind of foreclosure prevention program to make the president and the press happy. Larry and Tim didn't really care. They just wanted a good press release, not a good program. My heart still breaks looking back at that time period, when we had a new president with a strong commitment to helping families and a willingness to spend real money to protect them. Unfortunately, in my view, his advisors did not share his priorities. They cared more about the big banks.

And the big banks continued to fare very well under the new administration, with Tim calling the shots. Citi got its three bailouts. Any bank over $100 billion in size was assured that the government would bail it out. Tim and his allies even blocked our efforts to bring a new management team into Citi.

At my request our examiners were doing their own independent assessment of how healthy Citi's FDIC-insured bank was. I had completely lost confidence in the OCC. My examiners' report came back highly negative. Based on Citi's weak management and large amount of troubled loans and investments, they felt that its supervisory rating—a kind of grade that examiners give banks to reflect how much risk they pose to the FDIC—needed to be changed. Specifically, they felt that Citi's FDIC-insured bank needed to be put on what we called our "troubled bank list." This was a list we kept of the weakest banks, those that were in real danger of failing.

The two biggest problems our examiners identified at Citi were its weak management and lack of sufficient capital to absorb the big losses they would continue to suffer on their bad loans and investments. But as soon as the OCC and the New York Fed—now run by a man named Bill Dudley, a close ally of Tim's—found out about our examiners' plans, all heck broke loose. They were terrified that creditors and bank customers would run from Citi if they found out it was on the troubled bank list. We did not publicly identify the names of institutions that went on our troubled bank list, but we did publish the total number of banks on our list, along with their total assets. At that time there were 305 banks on the list, representing $220 billion in assets. If Citi's FDIC-insured bank went on the list, the assets would jump to $1.5 trillion. So even though we wouldn't release Citi's name, pretty much everyone would assume that it was on the list, as it was the only bank of that size in such bad shape. The OCC and the New York Fed argued that once Citi's investors and customers figured out that it was on the list, they would no longer want to do business with it, creating even more severe problems for the bank.

So here I was again, trying to do the right thing and treat Citi just like any other smaller bank, which would have been placed on the list long ago and ordered to change management and raise a lot more capital. That was standard procedure for small banks. On the other hand, forcing Citi onto the list, without the support of its primary regulators, could be very risky for the FDIC. What if the OCC and the New York Fed were right? What if investors and depositors "ran" from the bank, particularly Citi's many foreign customers who had hundreds of billions on deposit with it? If the bank collapsed, we would be forced to seize it to protect depositors. Without the cooperation of its primary regulators, this would be very difficult.

I decided to try to use the troubled bank list as a threat to get Citi to make changes. I told Citi officials that if they made significant management changes and increased the amount of capital the bank held, that might keep it off the list. The troubled bank list was updated every three months, so that gave us some time to get these changes from Citi before we would have to add its assets to the public troubled bank list. I thought it was a good plan, but here again, the OCC and the New York Fed fought us, as did Tim Geithner. They did not want to force any management changes at Citi, nor did they want to force it to significantly increase its capital. In fact, I felt they were letting Citi use accounting tricks to make its capital levels appear higher than they really were.

Fortunately, Ben Bernanke and a new Fed governor, Dan Tarullo, were more sympathetic to our position. With their help we did get several new board members who had substantial banking experience. Those members included Mike O'Neill and Jerry Grundhofer, two well-regarded former banking executives, and Diana Taylor, the former bank regulator for the State of New York. We were unable to immediately oust Pandit, but we did get the bank to hire an experienced banker to run that part of Citi that was FDIC-insured. We also replaced one of Pandit's top lieutenants. Eventually the

FDIC won. After a few years of experience working with Pandit, those new board members decided that he needed to be replaced, as we had long argued. So they gave his job to Mike Corbat, a respected Citi bank executive who had worked hard to get Citi cleaned up. Slowly but surely, the new board and management have improved Citi's condition, and today it is a much healthier, better-managed bank.

Looking back, I think the way Citi was handled says a lot about the flaws in bank regulation. There are many good, smart people who work at the OCC and the New York Fed, but I think at the top levels those agencies start identifying with the banks they regulate. Instead of seeing their jobs as protecting the public, they start seeing their jobs as protecting the banks. That was certainly the case here. The OCC and the New York Fed viewed their job as protecting Citi from the FDIC, much in the same way the OTS viewed its job as protecting WaMu from the FDIC. But our job was to protect depositors, not the bank, and when a bank's risky practices started to threaten depositors, we were obligated to act.

Tim did draw me into one more, final bailout. It was for a financial institution called GMAC, which was an arm of General Motors, the bankrupt car manufacturer. GMAC was originally founded to make loans to

people to buy GM cars, but in the early 2000s, it decided
it could also make a lot of money making subprime
mortgages. It formed a non-bank lender called ResCap,
which was in deep trouble. The Obama administration
had already decided that it was going to use TARP
money to help GM. But then Tim decided that we
needed to bail out GMAC, too, to make sure it was
still around to lend money to people to buy GM's cars.

There were valid reasons for the government to
help GM. Manufacturing is important to our economy,
and GM employed many people. The economy needed
those jobs. But asking the FDIC to get involved in
this was really beyond the pale. Our job was to protect
depositors, not bail out car companies. But Tim was
determined, and he summoned me and my staff to a
meeting in his office, where he told me he wanted the
FDIC to guarantee a lot of GMAC debt. He basically
threatened to attack me publicly. If I didn't agree to his
demands, he was going to tell everyone that I was the
one obstacle in the way of the GM rescue.

But because of ResCap, GMAC was also in danger.
Guaranteeing its debt would be very risky for us. And
here was the problem: If GMAC defaulted, the money
to cover the FDIC's losses would have to come from
other insured banks, including thousands of community banks. We had stretched our legal authority to

guarantee the debt of non–FDIC-insured banks like Goldman Sachs, Morgan Stanley, and GE Capital. But we had no legal authority to assess or tax those non-banks if we had losses. It would have to be paid by FDIC-insured institutions. I wanted a statutory change to let us slap assessments on these big non-banks if we had any losses. But Tim was resisting.

In the end, with the help of the White House chief of staff, Rahm Emanuel, we got our legislation, and knowing that I could tax these big non-banks if the FDIC lost money on GMAC debt, I agreed to guarantee some of it. Was this the right thing to do? I don't know. It really was far beyond the FDIC's mission. Throughout the crisis I always tried to meet my colleagues halfway and find a path forward, even with Tim! But even to this day, Tim and his allies criticize me for being "difficult" and "not a team player"—even after all the compromises we made. You just can't make some people happy.

GMAC, fortunately for us, was the last bailout. A non-bank lender called CIT gave us an opportunity to finally end them. CIT, which had about $100 billion in assets, was having big trouble. It had made a lot of risky real estate loans, and also used short-term, borrowed money to fund itself. For reasons I do not understand, it had convinced Hank Paulson's Treasury Department to invest $3 billion of TARP money, even though my examiners had warned that the lender was not viable. Then CIT came to us and wanted us to guarantee its debt. We said no. The debt guarantee program was only for solvent institutions, and we did not think CIT, even with TARP, was going to make it. So, guess what happened? With no bailout from us, CIT had to file for bankruptcy, and it was no big deal. Its shareholders and creditors had to take losses, but it emerged from bankruptcy as a much stronger institution.

I was so glad that we finally said no and nothing terrible happened to the economy. I was so tired of Tim and the other regulators constantly pressuring us to do bailouts, saying that if we didn't, the "system" would fail. "We have to save the system" was the constant mantra of our colleagues. At last, we let one fail, and the system did not go down.

Toward the end of 2009, completely out of the blue, Tim totally changed course on his seemingly endless willingness to give government money to nine banks. While less than a year earlier he had enthusiastically "ordered" the nine largest banks to take TARP capital, now he wanted all of them to pay it back. Many of the stronger banks had already repaid their TARP, but weaker ones, like Citi, and Bank of America (still reeling from its acquisitions of Merrill Lynch and

Countrywide), were not in a position to do so. So why did Tim suddenly want everyone to repay their TARP? In a word: compensation. Citi and Bank of America—because of the government's large, continuing investments in them—were subject to special restrictions on how much they could pay their executives and other high-paid workers. But if the government was repaid, they could get out of those restrictions.

We thought it was premature for them to repay. They needed every bit of their capital. But Tim insisted, so we negotiated an agreement that said they could repay TARP if they replaced at least some of it with new capital from investors. But once again, it was a huge fight with the regulators over how much new capital these banks needed to raise. We wanted Bank of America to raise $22.5 billion. The OCC and the New York Fed were happy with half that. We were able to get Bank of America to raise over $20 billion, so we won that one. With Citi, it raised $17 billion in new capital and paid back $20 billion. (As indicated earlier, they did not repay their remaining $25 billion of TARP. Rather, the Treasury sold those shares to other investors.) We thought Citi needed to raise $25 billion, but that was the best this weak bank could do. Investors were still fearful of it.

As these banks all exited TARP, guess what they

did? They paid almost all their top executives big bonuses that rivaled what they were getting prior to the crisis. (The exception was Vikram Pandit, who only got $1. Of course, he had already received nearly $200 million from previous bonuses and the sale of his defunct hedge fund.) The press coverage was terrible, and justifiably so. With so many people losing their homes and their jobs, these banks still didn't see anything wrong with paying big compensation packages. It made me wonder whether these government bailouts were about helping the "system" or helping the big banks with their bonuses.

As John Reed, the well-respected banker who ran Citigroup in the 1980s, said, "There is nothing I've seen that gives me the slightest feeling that these people have learned anything from the crisis. They just don't get it. They are off in a different world."

CHAPTER 12

2010–2011
THE POST-CRISIS YEARS

The year 2009 brought with it some victories— more capital into the banks, ending the bailouts, and securing legislation to make big banks pay for any losses on our debt guarantee program. But 2009 also had its frustrations. I felt the government was being far too generous in backing any banking institution over $100 billion. And government foreclosure prevention programs were providing very limited help for distressed homeowners.

As we entered 2010, new priorities and challenges emerged. The US Congress was moving forward with much-needed legislation to reform the financial system. My top priority was to get Congress to ban government bailouts of mismanaged financial institutions in the future. I was pushing them to instead establish a process to put large financial institutions into what we at the FDIC called "orderly resolution." Under this process—which we had used for decades for insured banks—the FDIC could take control of an entire large institution (including the non–FDIC-insured parts) and continue its basic functions—like making loans and processing payments—so that members of the public would not be hurt. At the same time, that process allowed us to replace boards and managers and force the institution's shareholders and creditors, not taxpayers, to bear the losses from the institution's mismanagement. The FDIC would force those shareholders and creditors to take responsibility for the institution's bad loans and investments, while bringing in new investors to provide fresh capital and stronger management to continue the healthy parts of the business.

This was basically the process that the FDIC had used with smaller banks, and it worked well. It made sure that there was no disruption in the provision of basic financial services that were necessary to our economy. But it also imposed accountability for mismanaged institutions where it belonged: with the boards, executives, shareholders, and creditors.

What's more, I had a powerful ally in convincing Congress to establish such an "orderly resolution authority": President Obama himself! There is a very interesting story about how this happened.

In his tenure President Obama became very upset about AIG, a badly mismanaged insurance company. AIG had made a lot of stupid bets on the US housing market. As discussed in earlier chapters, it had sold a kind of insurance—called credit default swaps, or "CDS"—to all sorts of investors who wanted to protect themselves against mortgage securities losing money and also against big financial institutions defaulting on their debt obligations. When mortgage securities started losing so much money, and big financial institutions like Lehman Brothers defaulted on their debt, AIG was obligated to make payments to investors who had bought this CDS insurance from it. It didn't have enough money to do so.

The Fed and the Treasury Department decided to bail out AIG in 2008. AIG was an insurance company, not a bank, so they didn't try to drag me into that bailout. Thank goodness! By early 2009, when President Obama assumed office, AIG had received $170 billion in bailout money and was 80% owned by taxpayers. Yet, with taxpayers taking all these risks to help AIG, guess what its senior executives did? They used that government support to pay $165 million in bonuses, mostly to the very blockheads that had gotten the company into

trouble. Not only that, but Tim Geithner knew about those bonuses, and didn't tell the president about them. The president read about them in the *New York Times*.

The news broke on March 16, 2009. Tim called me in the morning on that same day and asked me to come to the president's office—called the "Oval Office" for its shape. He said the president wanted to see me, but he wouldn't tell me why. When I got there, Tim and Larry were sitting on couches with their heads bowed. They looked like two schoolboys who had been caught playing poker with the school lunch money their parents had given them. The president looked pretty upset. Right away he asked me to sit down, and the first thing he said was, "Have you seen the headlines on the AIG bonuses?"

"Yes," I said. I had, and I was aghast. I didn't understand why the government hadn't just fired those employees when they had done so much to hurt AIG. There was some suggestion in the press that AIG executives had paid them so they would stay and help undo all the damage they had caused! That was like paying an arsonist to help put out the fire he started.

"Do you have any thoughts on how to stop these bonuses?" the president continued. I looked at Larry and Tim, their eyes still downcast. I wanted to say, "Yeah. Just fire them." But then I thought Tim would

start arguing with me, since he had tacitly approved those bonuses. I didn't want to waste precious time with the president on a fight with Tim.

So instead, I decided to tell the president about the process we used with smaller banks that allowed us to take control of the bank, fire the people that needed to be fired, and force losses on shareholders and creditors, not taxpayers. Why didn't we try to get Congress to pass legislation establishing this same kind of process for big financial institutions like AIG? The president liked the idea, and even Larry and Tim were nodding. After that, the president remained highly supportive of giving the FDIC authority to put large institutions into this bankruptcy-like process.

For a while even Tim worked constructively with us, though later we would get into spats over how tough the legislation would be. I wanted a complete ban on bailouts. He wanted to preserve the government's ability to bail out institutions, as it had done with Citi and AIG. Fortunately, on that issue Congress was on my side.

In July 2010 the president signed into law the Dodd-Frank Wall Street Reform and Consumer Protection Act. The law was named for the two men who headed the key committees in the House and Senate that wrote this important law: Congressman Barney Frank of Massachusetts and Senator Chris

Dodd of Connecticut. This law did many important things. It banned high-risk, speculative trading by large financial institutions with a provision called the "Volcker Rule"—named after its chief proponent, the legendary Paul Volcker, who had chaired the Federal Reserve Board from 1979 to 1987. And the law created a new government agency to protect consumers when they borrowed money, including homeowners. (Given the Fed's failure to write mortgage lending standards in the lead-up to the crisis, they lost their authority to write consumer rules.) Most importantly from our standpoint, a special section of the law, called "Title II," banned bailouts and gave the FDIC powerful new tools to handle the failure of large financial institutions without resorting to taxpayer bailouts. It also mandated the firing of key board members and executives who had contributed to a bank's failure, and gave the FDIC power to get back all the compensation that had been paid to them during the three years prior to the bank's failure. This was a huge victory for the FDIC.

We had other important victories. Dodd-Frank removed many of the limits on our ability to collect premiums from banks for their deposit insurance, and also shifted more of the burden to pay for deposit insurance to large institutions. It permanently raised the deposit insurance limit to $250,000, which would better protect small businesses and older Americans who kept their money in banks, including grandparents who had set up trust accounts for their grandkids. And the law included the Collins Amendment, sponsored by Senator Susan Collins of Maine, to prohibit regulators from setting capital requirements for big banks that were weaker than those applicable to small, community banking institutions. This was a direct assault on the Basel II rules we had blocked in the US but, unbelievably, the Fed and the OCC were still pushing. With the Collins Amendment, the much stronger capital rules that applied to smaller banks would serve as a minimum capital requirement for the big banks.

We were making progress against Basel II in the Basel Committee as well. A lot of things had changed since 2006 when I attended my first meeting in Merida, Mexico. Europe was paying dearly for Basel II. Its thinly capitalized banks had little capacity to absorb losses when the 2008 crisis hit, and government bailouts were required for a number of them. What's more, European banks had invested heavily in debt that had been issued by weak European governments. They did this because the debt paid high interest rates, and under Basel II they could use 100% borrowed money to buy that debt. This gave rise to a new problem—called the European "sovereign debt crisis." (Debt issued by a government is usually referred to as "sovereign debt.") Given the ability to so easily sell debt to European banks, a number of weak European governments—including Portugal, Ireland, Italy, Greece, and Spain—had themselves borrowed too much and were teetering on the edge of insolvency. And if those countries collapsed, so would the banks that had purchased large amounts of their debt.

All of this was imposing a serious drag on the European economy. With so much borrowing and investing in risky sovereign debt, Europe's major banks were not in a very strong position to keep lending. The difficulties European households and businesses had borrowing money reduced their ability to spend and invest. The same thing happened with the US economy. But because we blocked Basel II for most of our banks, and in 2009 forced them to raise a lot more capital, our banks were doing a better job of lending. They still weren't doing enough, but they were doing better than Europe.

Europe's problems meant that European regulators were under a lot of public pressure to reform the banking system. As a consequence there were many members of the Basel Committee who now wanted much stronger capital rules for big banks. These included the chairman of the committee, Nout Wellink, the head of the Dutch National Bank; Mervyn King, the head of the Bank of England; and Phil Hildebrand, the head of the Swiss National Bank. After lengthy discussions we were actually able to convince the committee to add a "leverage ratio," a new simpler and stronger limit on a big bank's ability to use borrowed money. This was what I had proposed in Merida in 2006. We strengthened the capital rules in a number of other ways. Once implemented, these agreements would require banks to raise hundreds of billions of dollars of new shareholder equity to reduce their reliance on borrowed money.

Of course, Dodd-Frank, like the new Basel agreements, still had to be implemented by all the regulators. Both Dodd-Frank and the Basel agreements required all the regulators to write rules applying them to the banks they regulated. I knew there was going to be a huge battle over implementation. Many of the big banks were very unhappy with the Dodd-Frank and Basel agreements on capital. They would try to water down these reforms as the regulators wrote rules to implement them.

When Dodd-Frank was passed, I had about a year left on my five-year term as FDIC chairman. I was determined to get all the rules done that I could. Many of the rules we could write by ourselves. Those included Title II "resolution" authority and all the rules dealing with deposit insurance. Others, like the Collins Amendment, required that the bank regulators act together.

I wanted to act fast because I knew that industry lobbyists would try to play a waiting game. They would try to slow all the rules down, thinking that as time passed, public anger over the bailouts would fade and there would be less pressure on the regulators to be tough. So I put together teams of staff who had specific accountability for the rules we were required to write under Dodd-Frank and specific deadlines they had to meet. The always-amazing FDIC staff rallied together, and I am proud to say that of all the rules we could do by ourselves, we finished them before I left. We were also able to convince the Fed and OCC (the Dodd-Frank law abolished the OTS) to finish the rules implementing the Collins Amendment before I stepped down.

I thought I was entering the home stretch of my five-year tenure at the FDIC. The economy was improving, bank failures had peaked, and the FDIC was doing its part to get much-needed reforms in place. We continued our push for foreclosure prevention, at least for banks where we had some authority, but the administration's hopelessly complicated programs were helping far too few families. I had been excluded from the board that the administration had set up to oversee those programs, so I had to get reports from a colleague, Mary Schapiro, the chairman of the Securities and Exchange Commission, which regulated securities markets. She would always wonder aloud why she was on that board, not me, given the FDIC's considerable expertise with loan restructuring. I wondered too.

One of the problems with loan modification efforts was that most of the "servicing" was done by large banks that had not hired enough staff to handle the millions of borrowers who were struggling to pay their mortgages, as we saw in Part 1. (Recall, servicers are those institutions who are responsible for collecting payments from borrowers and passing them on to investors. They are also responsible for minimizing losses through loan modifications when a borrower becomes troubled.) This was frustrating to me, but here again, because we were not the primary regulator of those big banks, the best we could do was try to push the OCC to make these big banks hire the staff that they needed. (I am happy to report that none of the smaller banks that the FDIC regulated had these kinds of problems.)

By September 2010 it became clear that the problems at the big bank servicers went far beyond the lack of adequate staff. At that time it was revealed in several press reports that most of the big servicers were foreclosing on borrowers without proving that they actually had the legal right to do so. When a servicer forecloses on a family, it must show that it owns the mortgage (or is working on behalf of investors who do) and has the legal right to foreclose on the house when the borrower stops paying. But these servicers were so dysfunctional, they had lost this basic paperwork. So they had told their low-level staff to swear on an affidavit (a legal document that is filed with a court) that the banks had this paperwork, when they really didn't! This was the big-bank equivalent of the "dog ate my homework" defense. They were having employees tell the courts that they really, really did have the paperwork, but they just couldn't produce it right at the moment.

This came to be known as the robo-signing scandal because servicers' employees would sign thousands upon thousands of these affidavits without even reading them. Like robots, they just kept signing one after the other. Looking back, as skeptical as I was about some of these big banks and their weak management, they still never ceased to shock me. How could they take someone's home away—a very serious thing to do—without actually knowing if they had the legal right to do so?

The robo-signing scandal became a huge controversy. A number of state and federal law enforcement officials started thinking about bringing lawsuits against the banks for presenting false information to the courts and taking people's homes away when they weren't entitled to. The banks, of course, argued that this was all a tempest in a teapot. They said that they really did have the right to foreclose and that the only people losing their homes were those who had not paid their mortgages for several months. The big banks' regulator, the OCC, also took that line of defense, trying to downplay robo-signing as just a bunch of technical mistakes in paperwork.

As far as I was concerned, even if the problems were just "paperwork," that didn't excuse the servicers' behavior. When borrowers would apply for mortgage modifications, the servicers would request hundreds of pages of documents (which they would frequently lose) and then deny the modifications if it wasn't all in order. So why should banks be able to do what they want, if they don't have all their paperwork in hand? And I suspected that robo-signing went beyond mere paperwork errors. I feared that there were many homeowners who had been wrongfully foreclosed upon, even though they should have received a loan modification because of the servicers' sloppy records (people like Imani's mom in Part 1).

I wanted to set up a special government tribunal to independently investigate every single complaint by borrowers who believed they had been wrongfully sent into foreclosure. This tribunal would also be empowered to make the banks pay money to borrowers who had been harmed. But the OCC was opposed to this idea. Instead, it suggested that the big banks hire consultants to review borrowers' files, and those consultants would decide whether borrowers were harmed and should be compensated.

Since the OCC regulated these big banks (and of course, had the backing of Tim Geithner), they prevailed. This was a stupid idea, and one destined for failure. These consultants were hopelessly biased in favor of the big bank servicers. The big banks paid them millions and millions in fees to do various kinds of work for them. There was no way they were going to be objective. I said at the time that the consultants were going to make more money out of this foreclosure review than homeowners would, and I was right.

This "independent foreclosure review" dragged on for over a year, until a man named Tom Curry became the new head of the OCC. Tom was a former Massachusetts banking regulator who had served on the FDIC board when I was chairman. He put a stop to this review when he found out that bank consultants had racked up nearly $2 billion in fees while not one homeowner, not one, had received any compensation.

Precious time had been lost on this review, and

homeowners still needed help. Tom and his staff hastily negotiated a separate settlement that required the banks to pay $3.6 billion in cash to homeowners and another $5.7 billion in other kinds of help, like forgiving overdue mortgage payments or reducing loan balances. The cash payments to individual families ranged from a few hundred dollars to a maximum of $125,000. This was probably the best the OCC's new leadership could do, given all the time that had been squandered with the bank consultants. These consultants still profited obscenely. About three of them ended up making $2 billion in fees for conducting reviews that pretty much produced nothing. One of the firms, called Promontory, which was headed by a man who used to run the OCC, collected half of that amount. That's right—one bank consulting firm collected a billion dollars in a process that was supposed to help distressed homeowners. This was truly government at its worst.

CHAPTER 13

TOO SMALL TO SAVE:
THE IMPACT OF THE CRISIS
ON COMMUNITY BANKS

The financial crisis had a devastating impact on Main Street families. It also resulted in hundreds of community banks failing. (Smaller banks, generally defined as those with less than $10 billion in assets, are referred to as "community banks" because their services tend to be mostly concentrated in one community.) To be sure, not all community banks were innocent victims. Many made mistakes and took risks that they shouldn't have. But many also fell victim to the worsening economy, which was beyond their control. As businesses collapsed and people lost jobs, they were unable to repay their loans, and the resulting losses caused many community banks to fail.

During my tenure at the FDIC, I oversaw the failure of 365 banks, the overwhelming majority of which were community banks. (As discussed in preceding chapters, we bailed out almost all of the big ones.) Though this sounds like a lot, we had nearly 8,000 community banks when I became chairman, so the small-bank failure rate was less than 5%. While a good number of big banks struggled, the vast majority of community banks survived the crisis. Not only that, but they did a much better job of lending during the downturn than did multi-trillion dollar megabanks. In my opinion, there were two reasons for this phenomenon: 1) community banks, being smaller and simpler than megabanks, were more customer-focused and easier to manage, so they didn't make all those stupid loans and securities and derivatives investments; and 2) they had stronger capital levels to absorb losses than the megabanks did.

The early community bank failures that we handled in 2007–2008—only 28, but up from 0 in 2005–2006—were almost all due to bad management. Many of these failures were thrift institutions that made risky mortgages. Many others resulted from smaller banks making loans in areas far away from them, where they did not understand economic conditions. For instance, we had a number of Minnesota-based banks that had made housing development loans in "hot" real estate markets like Florida and lost large sums of money when Florida's housing market collapsed and the builders could not complete the developments.

As we got into 2009 and 2010, mismanaged banks continued to fail, but we also started seeing more and more failures resulting from worsening economic conditions. Some of the banks hardest hit were specialized banks called "Community Development Financial Institutions," or "CDFIs," which were dedicated to serving low-income neighborhoods. Because the impact of the recession was most severe in those low-income neighborhoods, CDFIs had a larger number of borrowers who could not repay their loans than banks that served more affluent communities. Many CDFIs failed. Community banks that made loans in states where home prices declined significantly also failed in larger numbers. These states included Florida, California, Georgia, and Nevada.

As I discussed earlier, the Receiverships and Resolutions staff of the FDIC—those staff who handled bank failures—had been cut to the bone when I arrived at the agency in 2006. We had to work very fast to rebuild that staff. I also raised the premiums that we charged banks for their deposit insurance to increase the money we had available to protect depositors. In addition, I made it the top priority of our agency that no insured depositor in a failed bank would ever have to wait more than one business day to access his or her money. I promised to bump up bonuses for FDIC staff every year that we met that objective, and we always did.

Not that the dedicated staff of the FDIC needed much of an incentive to protect depositors. No depositor has ever lost a penny of insured deposits throughout the agency's eighty-year history. The paramount importance of protecting insured depositors runs deep in the culture of the FDIC. The FDIC was created to end the kind of massive depositor runs that crippled our banking system and economy in the 1930s. It is frequently cited by Republicans and Democrats, liberals and conservatives, as one of the most successful of the agencies created amidst the Great Depression.

Notwithstanding our perfect track record, we faced a lot of skepticism that we could handle all the bank failures that were escalating rapidly. By 2009 we were averaging more than 11 failures a month, reaching a total of 140 by the end of the year. In 2010 the average exceeded 13 a month, reaching a peak of 157 for the year. In late 2008 and early 2009 we were constantly defending ourselves against media criticism that we wouldn't have the money or staff power to handle the escalating failures. I will never forget sitting in the aisle seat of an airplane on my way to give a speech in San Diego in 2009, when a young man walking down the aisle stopped and asked me if I was the chairman of the FDIC. When I said that I was, he said loudly, "Holy cow, you must be out of money. They have you flying in coach!" I stood up and announced to the other startled passengers that we had plenty of money, and told them that I always flew coach on domestic flights.

I was constantly on television or the radio, promising depositors that their money was safe. In 2008 we had decided to launch a media campaign about deposit insurance, to remind the public about our perfect track record of protecting depositors. I think that campaign helped assure bank depositors that their money was safe and that the FDIC would protect them, no matter how bad things got. But it was a relentless, ongoing part of my job to be out on television or the radio every week, easing the fears of a nervous public.

One of the smartest things that we did to assure depositors (and one of the riskiest) was to let a film crew from the news show *60 Minutes* accompany our staff on a bank failure. The *60 Minutes* producers and one of its reporters, Scott Pelley, were very eager to report how a bank failure worked and capture it on television for the country to see. Pelley even made a special trip to Washington to discuss their request with me. I weighed the pros and cons carefully. On the one hand, the *60 Minutes* show was widely watched. If the closing went well, it would give comfort to bank depositors throughout the nation not to worry about the safety of their insured deposits. However, if there was any misstep, if any of the depositors panicked despite our efforts to reassure them, the show could backfire.

When banks failed, it was not a surprise. Our staff would closely monitor banks once they went on the troubled bank list. When it became clear the bank wasn't going to make it, we would schedule a closing— usually several weeks in advance. Shortly before the scheduled failure we would run a confidential auction, giving other banks that we insured the chance to bid on the failing bank. Over 90% of the community banks that failed, we sold to other community banks in this way. We found that this was the best way to make sure banking services continued in the community uninterrupted—by selling a failing bank to a healthy, strong one that wanted to maintain banking services to the community.

It was our practice to close banks on Friday. That gave us a full weekend to make sure the transition to the new owners went smoothly. We had scheduled a closing on February 27, 2009, for a bank called

Heritage Community Bank in Illinois. After consulting with my staff, I decided to let the *60 Minutes* crew film this failure. Yes, this was a bold move, but at the end of the day, I had confidence in our people and their professionalism to make sure the closing went smoothly, whatever problems might come their way. I've never been as proud of our FDIC staff than on March 8, 2009, when the *60 Minutes* show aired. At home with my family on Sunday evening, I watched our FDIC staff calmly and confidently take control of Heritage and transfer ownership to MB Financial, another Illinois community bank.

There was one panicked couple who showed up on Saturday morning, the day after the bank had been closed. Jim Hess and his wife, Audrey, came to the bank with an empty suitcase, demanding all of their money in cash. One of our FDIC veterans, Rickey McCullough, explained the closing process to them, that the bank was under new management, and that all of their insured deposits were still safely in the bank and readily accessible. With Rickey's reassurances, the frightened couple calmed down. In fact, the *60 Minutes* crew filmed them leaving the bank, with a still-empty suitcase in hand, singing the praises of the FDIC.

The *60 Minutes* broadcast was a huge success

for our agency. After that, the public came to view a bank failure as a non-event for them, which it was. We never experienced an insured depositor run, and always guaranteed seamless access to their money. Unfortunately, not all depositors were insured. Some had uninsured deposits in failed banks, and by law they were required to absorb some of the losses from the failure. Frequently, acquirers of failed banks would cover those losses for uninsured depositors, because they were typically valuable customers whom the acquiring bank wanted to keep happy. But not always. I remember one instance when the mother of a soldier in Afghanistan had deposited his life insurance proceeds in a failed bank. In another instance a policewoman had deposited the proceeds of the sale of her home in a failed bank. It made me angry that the law required uninsured depositors to absorb losses, when the government was bailing out almost all of the big banks. Big bank investors and creditors, including big bond funds, were in a much better position to absorb losses than a policewoman in Southern California.

But this was just another reason why I was so determined to end "too big to fail"—its fundamental unfairness against the "little guy." Our country was founded on the notion of a level playing field. That is, the same rules apply to everybody. We all have the same right to succeed or fail. But in 2008 and 2009 we ignored that fundamental precept of our democracy. Big banks and their shareholders and creditors were protected, while small banks failed and homeowners struggled. Our focus was always on trying to help "the little guy," whether by protecting depositors or trying to keep people in their homes. I think that is why the FDIC's reputation was enhanced during the crisis. People sensed that we were trying to help them. The people who used banks were our priority, not the banks themselves.

We received many awards and accolades because of our work during the crisis. I think the one I am the most proud of is the John F. Kennedy Profile in Courage Award. I took my daughter, Colleen, with me to that award ceremony, which was held at the John F. Kennedy Presidential Library and Museum in Boston. President Kennedy's daughter, Caroline, gave Colleen and me a private tour of the museum. Colleen, then nine years old, had read picture books about Caroline growing up in the White House and riding her pony on the White House lawn. Colleen was surprised when she met the now-adult Caroline. She had envisioned the young girl in her book!

Receiving the award was a moving experience for me. I have never thought of myself as particularly courageous. I just act when I think something needs to be done. As I said in accepting the award:

"We weren't trying to be significant or to do something great or even courageous. We were just trying to do something that seemed like basic common sense. But seeing what was happening, we couldn't stand on the sidelines and be insignificant and do nothing."

PART 3
YOUR FUTURE

CHAPTER 14

THE LINGERING EFFECTS OF THE FINANCIAL CRISIS

Six years after the financial crisis, the United States' economy continues to struggle. The amount of household wealth—that is, the value of things that American families own, like houses, stocks, and bonds, minus what they owe, like mortgages and other loans—has recovered to about 87% of what it was prior to the financial crisis. In other words, it has taken us six years to almost get back to where we were prior to the crisis.

But that 87% doesn't tell the whole story, because it reflects total household wealth for all families added together, and does not reflect how individual families are doing. In truth, most of the recovery has been in stocks and bonds, and most stocks and bonds are owned by very wealthy people. The major source of wealth for lower- and middle-income families—their homes—has been slower to recover. And because millions of these families lost their homes to foreclosure, they will not be able to benefit even as home prices rise again.

Most of the wealth recovered since the financial crisis has been concentrated among richer families. And of course, some of the biggest beneficiaries have been bailed-out banks and their executives, who are making profits and bonuses that rival what they were making prior to the financial crisis. On the other end of the economic spectrum, lower-income families have not shared in the recovery. One study showed that young families headed by African Americans or Hispanics have only recovered 31% of their wealth. Families headed by whites or Asians who have not completed high school only recovered 20.9% of their wealth.

Income—which differs from wealth in that it relates not to what people own but what they make—has also been slow to recover. Examples of income include wages, interest payments on bonds, and profits from the sale of stock. In fact, one study shows that 121% of income gains since the financial crisis have gone to the richest 1% in our country. How could they capture more than 100%? Quite simply because the bottom 99% have actually lost income since the financial crisis. That is, the top 1% took all of the income increases since the crisis, as well as a little more from the bottom 99%. Here again, a big reason the richest Americans have benefited is because they derive much more of their income from stock and bond investments, whereas the rest of us rely primarily on wages for our income, and real wages for most people have declined.

Lower- and middle-income families are not the only ones who continue to suffer financially. Our federal government's finances are also being stretched. The federal government funds itself primarily through taxes imposed on personal and business income. That is, people and businesses pay a certain percentage of their income to the federal government in taxes, and those taxes support the federal government's spending. However, when so many people lost their jobs and so many businesses started losing money as a result of the financial crisis, it reduced the amount of income the government could tax. At the same time, the government started to spend more money to try to get the economy going again and to help people who had lost their jobs. In 2008, at the onset of the recession, the government collected $2.5 trillion in tax revenues and spent around $3 trillion, creating a budget deficit of about a half trillion dollars. By 2009 tax revenue had dropped to $2.1 trillion while spending shot up to $3.5 trillion, nearly tripling the budget deficit to $1.4 trillion. Though the deficit started coming down somewhat after that, as the economy slowly improved, through 2012 it remained over $1 trillion a year. In 2013, it dropped to $680 billion.

What happens when the government spends more money than it takes in? How does it make up for this deficit? It borrows. It issues debt securities to banks and other investors in the US and, indeed, throughout the world, and promises to pay the money back later with interest. The total amount of money the government has borrowed and has not yet paid back is called the "national debt." At the end of 2007 the national debt was about $9 trillion. By the end of 2013 it exceeded $17 trillion. Both political parties bear the blame for the national debt, as both have made a habit of spending more than we collect in tax revenues. However, the damage of the financial crisis has made the problem much worse.

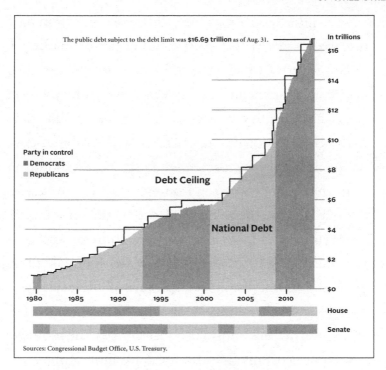

The public debt subject to the debt limit was **$16.69 trillion** as of Aug. 31.

In trillions

Party in control
- Democrats
- Republicans

Debt Ceiling

National Debt

House

Senate

Sources: Congressional Budget Office, U.S. Treasury.

This huge debt eventually will have to be paid back by future generations. If the economy improves substantially (a big if), we may generate enough in additional tax revenues to pay down this debt without increasing the proportion of people's income that they have to pay in taxes. More likely, however, future generations will have to pay higher taxes to keep the national debt at a manageable level. Making the problem worse is that older, retired people will continue to comprise a bigger and bigger share of the population, while those working and paying taxes will constitute a smaller percentage.

We already spend about 40% of the federal budget on two programs that primarily benefit older people: Social Security, which provides money to support older people in retirement, and Medicare, which helps cover the cost of health care for older Americans. According to the Congressional Budget Office (CBO), the amount we spend on these programs is about 2.5 times greater than the amount we spend on everything else besides defense. That is, Social Security and Medicare—known as "entitlements" because the government commits to older people that they will be paid—are 2.5 times greater than the combined amount of the money we spend on things like education, infrastructure, law enforcement, and energy development, things that make our economy more competitive and improve our quality of life. What's more, by 2021, about the time many of you will be entering the workforce and paying taxes, entitlement spending will have grown to 4 times the amount the federal government is spending on everything else besides defense.

Both Medicare and Social Security are funded by special payroll taxes that are set aside to pay for benefits under those programs. Both programs are "pay as you go," meaning that the special taxes paid by today's workers are used to support today's retirees. Right now enough money has been accumulated for both programs to cover all the benefits they are paying out to older people, but both programs are predicted to fall short in the not-too-distant future: Medicare by 2030 and Social Security by 2033. If nothing is done to fix the problem, Medicare beneficiaries would suffer benefit cuts of about 15% and Social Security beneficiaries would see cuts of about 25%.

Many people (including me) think that Congress should act now to deal with these funding shortfalls before they happen, but others think we should wait, particularly for Social Security. After all, they say, the economy could start growing a lot faster and create more and better-paying jobs, and this would increase the amount of special tax money going into the programs without Congress having to make hard decisions to increase tax rates or decrease benefits.

But it is more likely that our economy will not grow fast enough to make up for these predicted shortfalls. And if we wait, the pain for either workers or retirees or both will be much worse. Imagine that you ran the government in a country we will call Profligatia. Imagine further that your government was collecting $100 billion in taxes to pay for $100 billion in retirement and health benefits, but in ten years suddenly the taxes you collected would only be $90 billion and the benefits you had to pay would rise to $110 billion, for a $20 billion shortfall. What would be better? Wait until ten years are up, then slash benefits or raise taxes by $20 billion? Or would it be better to more slowly accumulate savings through some combination of small, gradual increases in taxes and reductions in benefits, spread out over the entire ten-year period?

By acting now, Congress and the president could ease the sacrifices that future workers or retirees will have to make when Medicare and Social Security funds fall short. But so far they have been unwilling and unable to act.

Regulators have also failed in their responsibility to meaningfully reform the financial system. The Dodd-Frank financial reform law gave them strong powers to tame crazy risk taking by big financial institutions and clean up the securitization market, their efforts—while not insignificant—have fallen short. They have toughened capital requirements for big banks, but still allow them to fund themselves with $95 of debt for every $5 of equity. They have finalized the Volcker Rule, which should curb some of the worst instances we saw of risky trading by big banks, but they also included many exceptions to this important rule. The new Consumer Financial Bureau finalized important protections for homeowners against unaffordable, exploding mortgages of the kind we saw in the lead up to the crisis.

But regulators have failed to reform the securitization market and the bad incentives it creates. In the face of heavy, special-interest lobbying, they backed down on a Dodd-Frank requirement to make securitizers pay for some of the losses themselves if mortgages they securitize default.

Though the regulators have worked hard—and the financial system is more stable than it once was—the modest reforms that have been put in place pale in comparison to the horrific damage caused by the financial crisis. Unfortunately, the regulators have been intimidated by the rough lobbying tactics of the financial services industry, and in many instances, Congress has pressured them to water down rules.

CHAPTER 15

YOU CAN
DO BETTER

So there you have it. The sad story of our financial crisis, driven by unbridled greed and shortsightedness. There were many complex factors that led to the 2008 financial crisis, but at its core, the problem was this: too much borrowing. People buying houses borrowed more than they could afford, and sometimes people bought multiple houses with borrowed money, thinking that they could resell them fast and make an easy profit. Big financial institutions—who should have known better—provided the money for these loans through the process of securitization. To make matters worse, lots of these big financial institutions also borrowed too much money, which they couldn't pay back when the housing market turned. Taxpayers had to bail them out.

Borrowing money is an essential part of any economy, and there is nothing wrong with borrowing if it is to buy something that a family or business really needs, and that they have the ability to pay back. Borrowing to buy a home is something that makes sense for a lot of families, as it gives them a secure place to live and the chance for increased wealth if the house becomes more valuable over time. Borrowing money to buy a car makes sense, for example, if it allows you to get to a better job that will pay more money. Similarly, borrowing to go to college makes sense if you earn a degree that will increase your earning potential after you graduate. Borrowing to start or expand a business makes sense if you have a good product or service and the know-how to run a business. By being able to borrow money, businesses can grow faster, creating jobs and goods and services that we use.

But when families and businesses start borrowing too much money—more than they can pay back—bad things happen. The financial crisis occurred because, frankly, people and financial institutions got greedy, thinking that they could make lots of quick profits on rising home prices. Of course, home prices could not go up forever, but the people borrowing money to buy houses, and the financial institutions providing the money for them to do so, lost sight of that important fact.

The 2008 crisis imposed terrible hardships on lots of innocent people, including people who had nothing to do with the housing craziness. And it was all completely avoidable.

The thing that bothers me most about the financial crisis is that the people who were hurt the most were the least guilty of doing anything wrong. Most of the big financial institutions that securitized bad mortgages and speculated in mortgage investments got bailed out by the government. Few bank executives lost their jobs. And many were receiving big bonuses again by 2009.

The real estate professionals who took out loans to flip properties were happy to walk away when they could no longer afford their mortgages, as they did not live in the houses and put very little, if any, of their own money into the purchase of them. In contrast, less sophisticated people, like Matt's parents, who lived in their homes and were victimized by unscrupulous mortgage originators, had to give up their homes and leave their neighborhoods, frequently after exhausting their savings in a desperate attempt to hang on to their houses. People like Jorge's dad, who did not participate in the housing craze at all, still lost their jobs when the Great Recession hit, a recession caused by big financial institutions who were in so much trouble that they could no longer do their jobs of making responsible loans.

Young people were perhaps the most hurt of all. They had to face all of the hardships brought on by the 2008 financial crisis. And their futures remain clouded in its aftermath, with the prospect of slower economic growth, lower wages, and the risk of higher taxes to pay for huge federal deficits.

We ran our economy into the ditch because greedy people wanted to make a whole lot of money fast. This is ironic, because history is full of examples of Americans who have succeeded not by making fast profits through speculation, but rather by creating or investing in things of lasting value. Take the late Steve Jobs, for instance, who founded Apple Computer. Jobs was famous for his disdain of short-term profit taking. Rather, his obsession was in making products that his customers would love—things like Mac computers, iPods, and iPhones. Because he was so singularly focused on making products that people would like, he succeeded. People bought Apple products in droves—making Apple, for a time, the most valuable company in the world.

Warren Buffett, the so-called "oracle of Omaha," became one of the richest men in the world not by trying to make quick profits on the latest fad or asset bubble, but by finding companies that made good products and services, buying the stock, and holding on to it for many, many years. He once famously said, "You should buy stocks you would be happy to own even if the market shuts down for ten years." In other words, his advice was to invest in companies that you wouldn't ever need to sell because they made quality goods and services that people would always want to buy and use.

Now that you have learned about the financial crisis, let me suggest a few ways that you can define a better future for your generation and those that follow:

Be a Good Business Person: If you enter into business, produce goods and services of real value. Build a business based on making your customers happy, not trying to trick them into buying things (or borrowing money) that they do not need or cannot afford.

Be a Good Consumer: It may take more time, but do your homework when you are making a big purchase or borrowing money for something that you really need. Try to find the best quality product. If you are borrowing money, talk to several banks and figure out which one really cares about you and your needs by giving you clear, easy-to-understand information about loans and their costs. There are plenty of businesses and banks out there trying to do the right thing, even if it might mean passing up the chance to make a short-term profit by selling you a product or loan with hidden costs and fees. As a consumer you can help them by finding them and giving them your business.

Be a Good Parent: Don't borrow more money than you can afford to pay back, and save as much money as you can. It's important for your family to have savings to fall back on if you unexpectedly lose your job. Try to save enough to help your kids go to college so they won't have to go deeply into debt. And don't risk important things like your home when some sharp-talking salesman comes by with a good-sounding offer. If you decide that buying a home is right for you, get a safe, affordable mortgage and concentrate on paying it down over time.

Be a Good Citizen: Our government also became shortsighted during the housing craze. Government regulators thought banks were healthy because they were making big profits for a time, without looking to the future and what might happen if home prices went down. Similarly, Congress pushed regulators to be lenient with banks, and continues to do so. More than three years since the enactment of Dodd-Frank and more than five years since the crisis, Dodd-Frank is only half implemented, and many members of Congress are trying to stop or water down key reforms. Our elected leaders in Washington are also being shortsighted in their unwillingness to make tough choices to deal with our long-term financial problems.

Some seem to be more worried about raising money for their next reelection than they are about protecting young people from huge tax burdens in the future and making sure that the financial system doesn't blow up again. So be informed about our government and its finances, and let your elected representatives know that you want these problems fixed.

Our country faces many problems right now, but I believe that we can and will do better. America is still a great nation. Winston Churchill, the legendary British statesman, reportedly once said about our country, "You can always count on Americans to do the right thing—after they've tried everything else." My generation tried to do things the wrong way—making money by speculating on rising home prices, without thinking about the longer-term consequences of our actions when home prices inevitably declined. Your generation can do it better—by having some sense of responsibility for the welfare of your and future generations, and by contributing to our economy not through speculation, but by creating goods and services of real and lasting value.

EXPLANATION OF KEY TERMS

Bank: Banks come in different flavors.

Usually when people refer to a "bank," they are thinking of a traditional bank that takes deposits insured by the FDIC and makes loans. This kind of bank includes two types: a "commercial bank," which makes a wide variety of loans to businesses and households, and a "thrift" (also called a "savings and loan"), which specializes in making loans to people to buy houses.

However, there is another kind of bank, called an investment bank. It doesn't focus on making loans the way a commercial bank or thrift does. Rather, it helps businesses raise the money they need through what is called a "securities" offering. Once securities (defined below) are issued, this kind of bank also helps people and businesses buy and sell those securities among one another. The people and businesses who buy securities are called "investors." Investment banks usually support their operations by borrowing from other big financial institutions instead of taking deposits from households like yours, as do more traditional banks. Universal banks are banks that provide both traditional banking and investment banking functions. They might provide insurance, too.

Financial institution: This is an all-inclusive term for any company or firm that is primarily engaged in the business of providing financial services. It includes commercial banks, thrifts, investment banks, and universal banks, as well as non-bank mortgage originators, insurance companies, and others.

Loan: A loan is simply money given to a person or business (borrowers) for a temporary period of time, with a legal agreement that the borrower will repay all of it by the end of that time with some extra money called "interest." Interest is usually expressed as a percentage of the money being lent. For instance, I might lend you $100, with an agreement that you pay me back after a year with 8% interest. At the end of the year you would pay me back $108—the $100 I lent you and the $8 in interest. Loan agreements can require that the loan be paid back in one lump sum (as in this example) or paid back in periodic payments. For instance, I could have asked you to repay the principal and interest in monthly installments of $9, which over a year would total $108.

Mortgage loan: This generally refers to a loan made to a homeowner with an agreement that if the homeowner fails to repay the loan, the lender can take the house away from him.

Mortgage originator: This could be a bank, or another kind of financial firm called a "mortgage broker," that works directly with an individual or family who wants to take out a mortgage. If the originator is a traditional bank, it might hold on to the mortgage and keep the repayments for itself. Or it might sell the mortgage to a securitizer, as explained below. Mortgage brokers generally sell the mortgages they originate. They do not keep them.

Securities: Households and small businesses usually borrow by going to a traditional bank and getting a loan. However, bigger businesses like to raise money in a different way: through a securities offering. These securities can take many forms.

For instance, the business may decide that it wants to sell off tiny ownership pieces of itself to lots of different investors. If the company does well and makes money, those investors will profit. If the company does poorly, those investors will lose money. These ownership pieces are called "equity securities," or more commonly, "stock" or "shares" in a company.

Another way that bigger businesses raise money is by issuing debt securities to lots of investors. These are like loans in that the business promises investors that if they give the business money now, it will pay them back later, plus interest. Unlike equity securities, where investors only profit if the company does well, debt securities have to be paid back no matter how well the company does. Governments also raise money by issuing debt securities.

Equity and debt securities have been around for a long time. A newer kind of security is called a mortgage-backed security. As discussed in Chapter 1, these are securities that represent the right to receive a certain portion of the money generated when homeowners repay their mortgages. Securitization got its start with big companies called Fannie Mae and Freddie Mac, which were authorized by the government to buy up mortgages, package them all together, and sell tiny pieces off to investors. Later, large institutions, primarily investment banks and universal banks, started doing the same thing. Fannie Mae and Freddie Mac guaranteed payments on the mortgage-backed securities that they sold to investors, but the big banks did not.

Securitizer: A financial institution that puts together and sells mortgage-backed securities.

Servicer: This is the firm that services a loan. If the mortgage was originated by a bank that kept the loan, it usually also services the loan. If the mortgage has been securitized, the investors who bought the mortgage-backed securities will hire a firm to collect payments from the mortgage borrowers and pass those payments on to the investors. Investors usually hire the big banks that securitized the loans to do the servicing.

Servicing: This is the process of collecting payments on mortgages and passing those payments on to investors when mortgages have been securitized. It is also a servicer's responsibility to work with borrowers who become late on their mortgages to try to get them current again on their loans. If the borrower stops paying his mortgage altogether, it is the servicer's responsibility to take the house away and sell it so that investors can get some of their money back.

INDEX